T0329184

Rethinking Irregular Migration

Causes, Course, Consequences and Corrective Measures

Seedy Drammeh

Published by CENMEDRA – the Centre for Media and Development Research in Africa

First published in The Gambia in 2018 by CENMEDRA
www.cenmedra.org

ISBN: 978-9983-960-16-7

Front cover design by Sadibou Kamaso
Layout design: Folashade Lasisi J W
www.cenmedra.org
info@cenmedra.org

Contents

Dedication

To migrants around the world, returnees from Libya and humanitarian agencies that promote the rights of migrants, particularly the International Organization for Migration (IOM).

About the Author

Seedy Drammeh is a Doctor of Business Administration, born in The Gambia in Jarra Sikunda, Lower River Region. He had his Primary education and Part of high school education in Jarra West before moving to the city of Banjul where he completed high school education.

He attended tertiary education at the Gambia Technical Training Institute (GTTI), before proceeding to the United Kingdom where he obtained his degree in Business Administration. Upon completion of his University education in 2003, he returned to the Gambia and joined the Customs & Excise Department as Assistance Collector.

Seedy was later appointed to the Position of Human Resources Manager in 2008 following the merger between the Customs and Domestic Tax Department in 2006. He served in the position of HR & Administration Manager for more than 8 years. He has undergone a series of professional training on Human Resources Management and Customs.

Seedy has strong passion for writing and has authored more than twenty seven books that are sold around the world.

Contact : + 220 9807933 / 3774317/ 7572507

Email : sdrammeh2009@yahoo.com

Acknowledgements

I would like to thank the International Organization for Migration (IOM) for standing by migrants in Libya and around the world and for speaking on behalf of vulnerable people in search of economic well-being and protection. As indicated by many returnees from Libya, the IOM played a crucial role in saving the lives of many young men and women, including minors who embarked on the perilous 'back-way' journey across the desert and got stuck in Libya in the hands of various gangs and bandits.

Similarly, I would like to salute the efforts of various humanitarian agencies, particularly Amnesty international, for advocating the freedom of people. Many humanitarian agencies have striven to ensure that migrants in Libya and elsewhere were treated with dignity. Equally, the crucial role played by the United Nations in promoting the dignity of migrants was commendable as it influenced decision-makers around the world to make policies that support fair treatment of migrants.

My profound appreciation goes to the new Coalition Government of The Gambia for their concern for Gambians around the world, especially the migrants who were stuck in Libya. It was clear that the Government of The Gambia made several efforts to ensure that Gambians and other nationals who were in Libya were safely returned home following the report of their maltreatment by various gangs and bandits in Libya. The government has consistently told Gambians that its citizens in Libya will be evacuated safely and it was wonderful that the government honoured its promise.

Also, the support from the diplomatic and consular corps in The Gambia in providing support towards the evacuation process and in making sure that the returnees were accorded dignity was tremendous. Parents continue to show their appreciation for the safe return of their children. It is clear that without the concerted efforts of various partners many more young men and women could have died in Libya in the hand of notorious gangs and bandits who extorted money from poor migrants.

Finally, I would like to openly express my sincere appreciation to the following colleagues at the Gambia Revenue Authority for supporting my many movements around the Greater Banjul Area to interview many returnees from Libya in order to get the true account of their experiences. Mr Alagie K. Mbye - Customs Manager at Banjul Seaport; Mr Ebrima Nyass -Customs Manager-Farafenni Customs Post; Mr. Saihou Jallow - Customs Manager; Mr Sulayman Sawaneh -Senior Customs Officer (Amdalai Customs Post); Mr. Bubacarr Bojang- Senior Customs Officer Basse Customs Post; Saihou Balajo-Senior Customs Officer; Mr Baba Fofana - Customs Officer at Customs Headquarters; Mr. Filly Dambelleh - Customs Officer I; Mr Alagie H Cham, Customs Sub-Officer III at Customs Post Airport and Yaya Jawo- Customs Guard-Giboroh Customs Post.

About CENMEDRA

CENMEDRA – the Centre for Media and Development Research in Africa – is a knowledge centre. Registered as an educational charity in The Gambia on 3 March 2014 it aims to promote, facilitate and disseminate research in media, communication and development in Africa. Its activities are focused on five main areas namely media research, researching development, new media and society, education, and publication. In line with its underlying aim of research application, it shares its research results with policymakers, media and development practitioners, media houses, regulators, scholars, politicians, librarians, activists, donors, development agencies, and the wider research community. It has a two-tiered governance structure: a board of trustees drawn from the media, civil society and academia, which provides strategy and policy direction, and an administrative secretariat that is responsible for operations and policy implementation.

MISSION
CENMEDRA exists to foster innovative research that puts Africa on the path of peace, progress and prosperity.

VISION
CENMEDRA envisions an enlightened African society, free from the burden of ignorance, where everyone is able to realise their fullest potential in peace and prosperity.

VALUES
Integrity
Openness
Creativity
Diligence

"There is only one good – knowledge, and one evil – ignorance."
Socrates (circa 470-399BC)

http://www.cenmedra.org
Email: info@cenmedra.org

Problems are solved by *thinking*, not by a special method.

(Adapted from Thomas, G., 2011, p.4)

Preface

The economic and political instability in many developing countries coupled with soaring unemployment rate among the youth and insecurity has compelled young men and women, including juveniles to embark on the perilous journeys across the Sahara Desert and the Mediterranean Sea to Europe. Although many of them reached their dream land, some perished along the way especially while attempting to cross the sea by ridiculous rubber and wooden boats. The developed countries and the international humanitarian agencies need to know that these vulnerable scores of people flee their countries for different reasons such as poverty, war, violence, intimidation, insecurity and persecution. They leave families and other loved ones behind in search of a better life and to be able to support their people back home.

Also, youth decide to leave their countries to embark on the dangerous irregular migration (known in local parlance as back-way journeys) because they are faced with the difficulty of getting employment. In fact, alongside the lack of protection and respect for human dignity in many countries, the level of unemployment was soaring at the time the youth population was on the increase. Despite having talents in various professions and relevant education, many youth got frustrated because they lack decent jobs. Even the category that got employment was faced with the difficulty of supporting their families due to the very low income they earn. It is because of the low income that they find it hard to have good basic human needs such as good food, shelter and medical care. As the youth continue to battle with survival they are constantly faced with the challenge of providing support to their extended families that depend so much on them for feeding, shelter, medical care and paying school fees for children.

It is a fact that many youth in the developing countries have acquired relevant education up to university level but with all their qualifications many of them remain unemployed due to lack of job opportunities. Besides the category of youth who have completed school, there are many other highly-skilled categories of youth who have acquired knowledge and abilities in various jobs such as carpentry, welding, masonry, tailoring, plumbing etc., but are unable to fully support themselves and their families because of the low income they earn. Truly, the youth are attached to their professions to the point that they rarely have time for themselves but with all that they got frustrated for not earning a decent income.

The lack of employment in most developing countries has got to a point where many educated youth are forced to take up casual work no matter the pay because they want to support their families. This is the reason you find educated youth doing fishing, timber logging, transportation of goods on donkey and horse carts for a pay, transportation of good on wheelbarrows, particularly around market areas for a pay, cleaning offices, working in women's garden for a pay and even selling firewood. To know this you only need to move around the developing countries and see for yourself how the youth are battling with survival despite their education.

These people are committed to work and earn a decent income for living but they are faced with unemployment due to lack of job opportunities in most developing countries coupled with low pay for the few jobs available on the job markets. Alongside the economic hardship is the frequent political misunderstandings created by the politicians that always result in violence forcing people to migrate as refugees and internally displaced people. The economic frustration and political instability in many developing countries are what force people, particularly the youth, to embark on the perilous 'back-way' journeys in search of sanctuary and economic well-being in Europe and elsewhere in the developed world. Let African leaders and their partners in the developed countries understand that the youth of the Africa can only stay home when the African continent is stable politically and economically. This means having employment opportunities and protection of human dignity at all times.

Seedy Drammeh
Banjul
3 March 2018

Introduction

The move by the European Union to reinforce more naval forces in the Mediterranean Sea in order to deter the movement of would-be migrants to their land was not the solution to the influx of people who are in search of protection and economic well-being. Seriously, the campaign to stop people risking their lives in the Mediterranean Sea with the aim of reaching the Promised Land should focus on studying the root causes of the mass exodus of people through the 'back- way' across the dangerous desert and sea. It is on record that after the European Union –Turkey deal aimed at stopping people using short routes to Europe the number of people who risked their lives on longer routes through Libya across the Mediterranean Sea has increased despite the heavy presence of naval forces.

It should be noted that most of the people who use the 'back-way' journeys across the desert to Libya are mainly from failed states. Most of these people know the danger of using the 'back way' but because of poverty and insecurity in their country they risk their lives to reach Europe in search of protection and a better life. They remain committed to pursue their dreams despite seeing some of their colleagues perishing along the way. Speaking to some of the returnees made me know that some of them knew very well that Libya was unstable prior to their departure but went ahead nonetheless convinced that it was the only way for them to achieve a better life. They took the risk because they are frustrated by the high-level of unemployment, poverty, lack of security and intimidation from tyrannical leaders who ruled their countries.

In the case of The Gambia, many young men and women from almost every family embarked on 'back-way' journeys to reach Europe through Libya. The mass exodus of the young men and women was caused by a number of factors such as poverty, persecution, insecurity, peer influence based on remittances from abroad as well as lack of respect for them in society due to their inability to look after their families. To confirm this, I embarked on a tour of different parts of the country reaching hamlets, villages and towns and the tour enabled me talk to many people asking them about their views of poor guys. While the majority of the people I spoke with have little or no respect for poor guys because they think their poverty is their fault and nobody should even think of giving them their daughter to marry, other people think to be successful and get respected requires one to go to Europe. No matter how hard it was for me to digest their thoughts, I believe they have a point considering the fact that most beautiful buildings, good businesses and nice cars are either own or financed by people leaving in the diaspora.

Even though some people never got successful in the past considering the fact that they left the Gambia in search of greener pastures and eventually stayed abroad for many years without returning home, yet young men and women are determined to go abroad because of poverty and insecurity. Despite the fact that some unsuccessful people from the diaspora, mainly African countries, shared their bitter experiences on the 'back-way' journeys, the young men and women have continued with their desire to reach Europe and elsewhere through the 'back-way' journeys. They regularly say that they would like to have their own experiences before they could believe the stories other people are telling them. Obviously, most of the young men and women either know or have heard about someone who left for abroad and never returned after many years yet they are committed to having their own experiences.

I saw people who left the country during our childhood in search of greener pastures but never returned successful after many years of having been away. Sadly, they found that the majority of their loved ones have died, while others have relocated to different places. It is always a very sad story that usually left such people in trauma for long time, especially where the persons who passed away happened to be their biological parents who had done everything possible to see them successful. Nonetheless, poverty and insecurity compelled young men and women to embark on similar journeys because they want to be respected and build nice houses. It should be noted that migrants contribute significantly to the economies of their host countries by paying taxes from the casual jobs they do, as well as their home countries by sending remittances that take care of feeding, school fees, medical care and construction of solid structures.

Disrespect for the poor in many developing countries has got to a point where the presence of a poor elderly in family discussions is not given a high regard as long as the rich guy is present irrespective of his/her age. It is the rich guy whose words are valued as long as he or she contributes financially to the survival of the people. Besides lack of respect and recognition even by their own siblings, the poor guys are usually the ones viewed as bad people in the family. I have seen a number of situations where poor guys were always the primarily suspects anytime something valuable gets missing in the house. Seriously, our society has got to a point where it is only a few religious persons who value poor guys.

These and many other things, including the worsening political and economic instability in most African countries are the factors that make people risk their lives through the 'backway' to reach Europe.. The political instability usually results in unnecessary civil or tribal conflicts. Because most politicians like to grab power no matter what it takes: they sponsor some greedy and disgruntled people to fight their political opponents when they feel insecure in their position. These unnecessary conflicts only cause loss of innocent lives including women and children. Many people usually get killed and the lucky few survivors normally find their way out in search of protection.

With all these available facts the developed countries instead of reinforcing their naval forces in the Mediterranean Sea to curb the movement of migrants should focus on promoting economic and political stability in Africa to help people have their liberty and stay home. Evidently, everyone knows that the search for greener pastures has always been part of human survival and will continue so long as inequality exists. What people need to advocate is equality and stability so that the respect for human dignity will remain uncompromised. The campaign for economic and political stability in Africa needs to start now.

1

The Root Causes of 'Back-Way' Migration

Africa is mourning as the continent's young men and women die in the Mediterranean Sea as they attempt to reach Europe using wooden and rubber boats. The number of lost lives of vulnerable African youth in the desert and the Mediterranean Sea has put almost every family in Africa in deep pain with many parents in total sadness. The mass exodus of youth through the 'back-way' journey began like wild fire spreading rapidly and affecting virtually every family at least in The Gambia. Truly, the mass movement of youth was extraordinary considering the number of people that left within a short period of time. It is obvious that like people from other continents, Africans have always had the feeling of moving to other parts of the world to explore opportunities but the mass exodus that made the continent's young men and women move through the 'back-way' journeys in search of protection and economic opportunities was unprecedented.

Towns, villages and hamlets were virtually empty due to the absence of many youth who embarked on 'back-way' journeys across the desert to reach Europe. Seeing the huge number of young men and women leaving day by day mainly on buses made me worry about the future of the African continent. My worry was not just limited to the brain drain but also the loss of possible successors of the continent of Africa. The future generations of Africa are in hurry to grab wealth because of frustration due to poverty, insecurity and oppression. The root causes of the frustration are lack of respect and recognition in society due to lack of money as well as denial of basic human needs such as status and right of belonging. The majority of the people in African seem neglected while the minority African elites scoop the natural resources of the continent at the expense of the vast majority. Because the national cakes are being shared by the minority elites of the continent the unprivileged majority are left with absolute frustration.

While the poor majority live in a constant state of fear due to lack of access to wealth and intimidation by the powerful guys, the minority elites continue to fight over power thus causing civil wars that only make the unprivileged devastated. They create segments referred to as political elites and decide who should do what in their interest. Within the segments are sub-divisions that are equally headed by the same greedy people who only care about their interests. These divisions and mismanagement of national cake make the poor suffer more. As the teams leaders realize that the sub-division heads are getting conscious they embark on struggle for total control of power and wealth. Unfortunately, the move leads to more division and so the fight for superiority arises. It is through this struggle that conflicts occur, which in turn leads to civil wars that continue to take the lives of innocent and vulnerable members of the African society.

Though Africa's problems are caused by Africans, I believe the developed countries can help remedy the problems by engaging their partners on the continent. Unmistakably, most African leaders get networks with the West to enable them to rule their countries and it is the western powers that influence the success of the networks they can engage African leaders on the need to maintain peace and create opportunities for their people such as employment and security. The development projects given to African countries by the developed countries and international agencies should be monitored thoroughly to ensure that the people of the continent benefit instead of the few elites.

Let the developed countries know that apart from the continued economic hardship endured by the majority of poor Africans, the mass exodus movement of the people through the 'back- way' journeys is reinforced by political instability and deliberate denial of people's rights by most African leaders. In order to fully establish the reason for 'back-way' movement the world has to study the root causes of the exodus movement of poor people. This could be done by looking at case by case. The move will enable the world to know that while some people leave Africa due to their poor state of living in their countries, others leave due to civil wars, insecurity, intimidation and lack of access to medical care.

Learning from history, I got to understand that migration has been a long phenomenon that existed over millions years ago. It will certainly continue to occur so long as inequality, insecurity, poverty, persecution, war, drought and hunger exist. I recall that in my childhood a number of people left our village in Jarra Sikunda and the surroundings for overseas in search of greener pastures. Sadly, after almost forty years, some of them still have not returned home and have not done anything to change the living conditions of their people. A few of those old travellers eventually returned home empty-handed and are sharing their bitter experiences with the young. It is these people who continue to tell the young people that some of those who did not return could not make it and have decided to get married and settle in the country they are. This is a very sad story considering the desire they had for helping their families at the time they were leaving.

In fact, we now know that the majority of the old travellers from the village and its surroundings never reached Europe or America; instead, they ended up living in some African countries that do not have strong economies. No doubt this is a very sad story; considering the fact that many of these people left their wives and children behind for many years. I have seen situation where the father returned after thirty years of being away and could not recognize the only child he left behind at the age of two. Also, there are a number of situations where people returned and found that many of their loved ones died including their biological parents that struggled hard for them. Despite the shared bitter experiences of the first travellers the young generation of Africa remains more committed to leave the continent through the 'backway' to unknown destinations because they lack confidence at home where unemployment soars.

Migration is simply defined as the movement of people or group of people from one geographical location to another mainly across national borders. These people often have the intention of temporarily or permanently settling in a country other than their native country. History has taught us that human beings have been moving from one country to another in search of resources, knowledge and other opportunities. However, the movement of people has taken a new dimension since middlemen have taken the role of facilitating the movement of people by asking huge sums of money as compensation. The middlemen continue to act dubiously by ripping off the poor migrants with false intentions of helping them reach their destinations safely.

In order to know the root cause of the mass exodus of people from Africa through the back-way journeys to Europe you need to ask how it all started. Firstly, looking around almost every village, hamlet and town in most parts of Africa and seeing beautiful houses, cars and other properties said to be owned by people living in the diaspora you will realize that the people are in serious competition. Also, lots of young men and women get influenced by their peers most of whom when they come home on holiday start to behave differently. It is always interesting to see how some people living abroad referred to locally as "Semesters' behave when they come with cars and other valuables. These are the people who show off and even play music loudly wherever they are especially when they meet a group of young men and women. Because they behave that way, they make their home-based peers believe they should also strive to enter Europe and become somebody. Other people decide to leave after they see their colleagues in diaspora change the lives of their families by providing them better shelter, education, good food, medical care, fancy electronic equipment such as satellite dishes, television, smartphones and good cars.

Despite the naughty behaviours of some of the semesters, society gives maximum respect them, while it looks down on those living around them at all times. The semesters are respected as long as they continue to give money and make financial contributions to village matters something the majority of the local cannot do because of lack of money. In fact, even though some of them behave irresponsibly most of the semesters easily get whatever they want including beautiful girls to marry, an opportunity that is often hard to come by for the home-based youths. Obviously, there are also good sides of the story and that is to do with semesters who behave responsibly when they in town. The actions of such people inspire lots of other responsible home-based guys who usually endeavour to emulate them for doing good things. The responsible and caring semesters usually acts maturely and in many cases they contribute to the development of their communities. Such people normally spend their holidays wisely either by engaging in construction works such as building structures for their families or projects that would benefit lots of people in their localities. Because they do good things their actions influence others to look for opportunity to be in Europe so that they too can do similar things for their families and communities.

Talking to the responsible semesters could in many ways make you strive for a chance to get to the developed countries in order to seek a better life. They will tell you the true picture of Europe and elsewhere in the developed countries and at the same time give you advice that when making the decision to leave in search of greener pastures you should not think there is silver and gold waiting out there. They tell you clearly that it is only through hard work that you could make it and support your family. However, the stories of challenges and hardships in the diaspora do not change the desires of young people to reach Europe because they are frustrated and desperate. While some people have different views of migration, they should understand that some people have genuine reasons for leaving their countries, including the desire to change the lives of their people for good. They could have done this back home if there were opportunities such as good employment and job security.

It has been decades since the people of African continue to struggle on their tiny farmlands and orchards in order to build good houses and put good food on the tables but they never realize their dreams due to many factors such as poor economic status of their governments and lack of markets for their products despite the hard work. It is important to understand that the people are working hard but because the opportunity to earn better is not available they almost end up working for nothing. It is sad that despite their immense hard work, the African farmers get poorer by the day while the rich are getting richer from the hard work of the poor farmers. Africa is a continent where the farmer struggles all around the rainy season and after harvest cannot get a better market for their produce. In fact, it is the middlemen who make more money out of farm produce than the farmers. To know this fact you need to travel in most rural areas of Africa and see how much the poor farmers sell their produce to middlemen who normally transport the produce to city where there is a ready market only to double the price of produce thus earning three or five times more than the poor farmers who worked for it.

Travelling around the rural areas of most African countries will enable you to see fresh vegetables that the poor women gardeners struggle to cultivate for months only to end up selling at a giveaway price to a middleman because there is no storage facility to keep their perishable produce for long and no market nearby where they can easily sell the produce. Because the farmers continue to live from hand to mouth they cannot build better houses and put good food on the table for their families. It is also the reason many farmers live in huts while the hard-working women continue to battle with their health as they do not get proper medical care. Because the poor famers live in that situation their ambitious children have no option than to risk their lives in order to assist them. This frustration also contributes to the mass exodus of young people through the 'back-way' journeys to Europe and elsewhere around the globe.

It is sad that while people leave with good intentions to help their people back home, some of them get killed in the desert and the Mediterranean Sea, while others never realize their dreams of returning home successfully as they get stuck in Libya where they face serious inhumane treatment. Because the few that were lucky to reach Europe usually return home on holiday during which they support their families, including building new houses, the home-based guys continue to nurse the ambition to follow their footsteps despite the stories of bitter experiences on the 'back-way' journeys. In fact, the competition begins immediately one successful returnee is able to change the living conditions of his/her family. This is the reason young men and women continue to have the dream of going to Europe and other developed countries around the world. It is important to know that it is not everyone who leaves for abroad wants flamboyant live; instead some have genuine reasons to struggle as they have the intentions to change the lives of their people.

Another factor that forces young men and women to embark on the perilous 'back-way' journeys was lack of job opportunities in their countries. Africa has the fastest growing population in the world and youth form the large portion of the population. Most of these youth have completed their secondary and tertiary education but remain unemployed. Because they cannot get employment they are forced to embark on these dangerous journeys in search of a better life. This is the case because most African countries do not have the capacity to create employment opportunities for their people. Not only are the governments unable to create office jobs, they are also unable to create manufacturing industries that can employ lots of people. It is the case because most politicians around Africa are interested in enriching themselves and their associates than thinking about creating opportunities for the citizens. It is the reason the continent cannot develop despite the mass acquisition of education and skills by the youth.

Looking at the root causes of irregular migration you will know how the families of the poor would-be migrants in Europe are getting poorer, while their children embark on journeys in search of a better life. It is a fact most of the people who embark on the dangerous journey through the 'back way' either sold their lands, animals or even jewelry of their parents. The exodus of the youth to reach Europe has got to a point where young men and women can take any precious items away from their parents and sell it only to make some good money for the 'back-way' journey. There are many families that have lost almost all their lands in the city because they sold them and gave the money to their children to go through the 'back way' with the hope that when they make it in Europe the family would get a better land to live on. Sadly, many families never realize their dreams as their children get perished in the Mediterranean Sea.

The sad memories of the 'back-way' journey will remain with many families in Africa for life as the continent has lost thousands of its youth in the Mediterranean Sea. In fact, there are some families that have lost more than two people in the Mediterranean Sea. Apart from the loss of lives, these families are virtually left with nothing because they sold all their valuables including land to support the journey of their children through the 'back way'. Although many children died and there are stories of other getting beaten in Libya, young men and women continue to go through the 'back way' because of economic and security reasons. While parents and governments are struggling to end the move, I urge the African society to change their view of poor guys to enable all people to live in dignity. It is a fact that poor guys in their communities are despised, while people with some money are the only respected ones who are usually listened.

Lack of regard and respect for the poor guy was a huge contributing factor to the massive 'back- way' movement by young men and women. It is a fact that in most African countries people have little or no regard for the poor, including their own families. There are situations where the young guys with money are valued more than even the elderly poor guy irrespective of whether they are from the same parents. Each time a family gathering happens it is the young rich guy that gets attention anytime he makes contributions during decision-making, while anytime the poor guy makes proposals no one pays attention to him. It has got to a point where poor guys find it difficult to get things like wife because it is almost seen as irresponsible to give wife to a poor guy. Because of the difficulties they face in getting their basic human needs, the poor are usually the primary suspects anytime something valuable get missing in the house. They are usually labelled as thieves, hypocrites and backbiters even when they behave responsibly.

This condescending treatment of poor guys does not commensurate with the African philosophy of Ubuntu (you are someone because of others; interconnectedness). Instead of concentrating on the material world our ancestors valued human beings. They respected each other and the elders were always given their due, particularly in family matters. The move helped them to strengthen family ties, which paid dividends as they built foundations for our generation despite the shift in direction. It is sad that the present generation shifted from the doctrines of their ancestors and took a new trend that only creates problems and disintegration. Let people know that it is because of the spiteful treatment of the poor guys that many young men and women have to embark on the perilous journeys with the aim of getting greener pastures. It is shocking to know that poverty and the concept of a poor guy have destroyed family ties, relationships and continue to make life hard for people without money in most African societies. Because the poor guy live on daily trauma he/she has no choice than to struggle madly for wealth even if means dying in the Mediterranean Sea.

While the poor Africans are struggling to survive in difficult circumstances, there are reports that despite entering Europe after risking their lives it is only a few migrants who have better living standards abroad. People always complain of hardship in asylum camps around Europe despite the maltreatment they experienced on the 'back-way' journey. Other migrants I spoke with told me that they went through a series of problems at the initial period of their stay in Europe. Some migrants continue to tell people back home of the racism and the unequal treatment they experienced in some European countries. With all facts stated about some of the reasons people risk their lives to reach Europe; I think the developed world should shift the campaign to stop irregular migration to Europe to focusing on promoting economic and political stability in Africa. While Africans are not blaming the developed world they want them to understand that it is only when Africa gains economic and political freedom that her children will live to stay on the continent.

Let all human beings understand that people primarily move from one location to another from various reasons. History teaches that previously people were compelled to move due to war, trade, pilgrimage, famine and drought and even some man-made disasters such as ethnic or tribal conflicts. The fact of the matter is that the same conditions keep forcing people to migrate. It is the reason migration must be considered a multidimensional phenomenon. The mass exodus of African youth should be viewed as the movement of poor people in search of protection. They move across political boundaries simply because they want a better life. They move because of lack of unemployment opportunities, deepening poverty, and absence of the right to economic opportunities that could help them support their families.

In order to deal with migration decisively there has to be an understanding of circumstances that compel people to leave their home countries such as unemployment, drought, war and even lack of recognition due to poverty. Of course, there are other factors such as good conditions found in Europe that attract people living in Third World countries. Obviously, the reasons for irregular migration vary from one person to another and from one community to another. If someone asks the reasons people migrate out of their native countries to unfamiliar locations, the answers will undoubtedly vary with causes found in such diverse factors as natural pressures, economic incentives, mental motivation, and political situation or civil war.

Africa has increasing population growth which influences both internal and external migration due to population pressure, poor harvests due to land degradation as well as civil wars that usually arise due to misunderstanding among politicians as they struggle for power. Another factor for migration is food shortages, hunger and malnutrition coupled with lack of proper medical care. Also social, economic and non-economic reasons are many and vary within countries that include the desire for quantifiable gain or food, the search for political or economic freedom and stability of the mind. While people are moving for various reasons, the world needs to know that migration is one of the ways in which the exchange of talents, services, skills, and a wider diversity of experience is obtained. Instead of looking at the bad side alone the developed countries should see the good side that continues to enrich other cultures.

It is sad that many young Gambians and other nationalities get perished in the Mediterranean Sea as they attempt to cross over to Europe. Many of these victims as indicated in various reports are young men and women who are mainly forced to leave their countries due to poverty and lack of security. It is unfortunate that these people die while struggling to support their families. However, the huge dead toll reported at the Mediterranean Sea does not deter people from embarking on 'back-way' journeys because they can longer cope with poor economic situations in their countries of origin. Apart from the loss of lives in the Mediterranean Sea there are reports that many of these people are subjected to lots of inhumane treatment in the hands of illegal brokers and private employment agencies mainly in Libya prior to their departure. The majority of them have gone through exploitative working conditions in Libya.

Besides the trouble migrants encountered on the 'back-way' journey across the desert and Libya, many of them also face the difficulty of getting proper employment in Europe. Because they usually arrive in Europe and other parts of the world almost empty-handed, they find it hard to wait for a long time to get employed through the legal employment agencies and so they usually use the illegal channels due to quick services rendered by those brokers. Such agencies take advantages of them by paying less money that usually puts migrants in trouble as they cannot put enough food on table and at the same time pay high bills. However, migrants normally prefer to live in that situation than to return home knowing very well the high expectations people back home have of them. Relocation to Europe in search of a better life has got to a point where it is almost seen as taboo to return home irrespective of whether one stays long in Europe or not. This applies to all categories of people including those who are studying and upon completion decide to return to their home countries. Each time a person returns home after living in Europe he/she is usually viewed as aimless especially where the individual return without lots of money.

2

Poverty and Remittances as Factors Responsible for Migration

It is this high expectation that is forcing migrants to take up all kinds of casual jobs so as to send remittances back home despite their low living status. Remittances are one of the most important things expected from people in the diaspora. It is the reason most migrants remit their little earnings through officials and non-officials channels and the move continues to give the impression to lots of people back home that there is lots of money out there. Remittances contribute to the economic status of the developing countries, far more important than official development assistance. Remittances continue to be received even at the time when most host countries are experiencing weak economic performances. According to the announcement made by the Office of the President of The Gambia, remittances contribute significantly to the economy of the country as well as economic well-being of families around the country.

I can say for certain that the bulk of development projects in The Gambia are funded by remittances from Europe and America. It is also used by families to place good food on the table, pay school fees, electricity bills, and medical bills and construct better shelter. Remittances have also changed the status of lots of people in terms of getting respect and recognition in society. It is used to buy nice cars, electronic gadgets and decorative items at homes. Remittances help families to regain their lost glory in terms of status and general conditions of living as the money is used on materials that transform people's way of life. Though Africans know that remittances from Europe and America cannot solve all their economic problems, they appreciate what is being sent, as it adds value to their lives.

The developed countries need to know that the only way to minimize the movement of Africans across political borders is to support African countries economically. As long as Africa is unable to get out of problems such as, war, diseases, poverty, chronic corruption, lack of employment, access to credit facilities, lack of access to markets, lack of entrepreneurial development programmes, political and economic instability the issues of people moving in search of a better life will not stop. The fact about migration is that people in need of protection and economic well-being will continue to leave one geographical location for another until and unless their governments are able to develop and implement policies that really reduce insecurity, violence and poverty, tackle corruption and strengthen institutions to enable people to have their say and enjoy their share of the national cake.

The developed countries need to accept people in need of protection and at the same time work with the developing countries to address the root causes of migration. It is important to know that people are fleeing their countries for various reasons. In many cases they face real and specific threats of hunger and starvation, violence and segregation because of poor economic status. Also, in many marginalized communities women and children are victims of abuse, rape and murder and because they cannot stand up and fight they run away to get protection elsewhere. Like other parts of the world, many people were previously forced to leave Africa as they feared arrest and torture by the autocratic rulers that went after people who did not support their political ideology.

Also, lack of society's approval of the economic status of young men and women is another driving force responsible for 'back-way' migration. To understand this better, I spoke with lots of young men and women who have risked their lives through the 'back way' but were unable to make it after all the hardship encountered in the desert and Libya. Out of the many young men and women that shared their story, one Karamo Ceesay a native of Tallinding in the Greater Banjul Area said he began his journey with only seven thousand dalasis on him (approximately US$120). The money, according to him, was obtained from the sale of the only family land. According to him, he sold the land without the approval of the other family members. He said he did that because he knew his family wanted him to stay in The Gambia and manage with the little earnings he had. Acting stubborn, he refused to listen and paid a boat that transported him to Senegal where he met nationals from other countries in the sub-region. According to him, they stayed in Senegal for four nights after which they paid for a train to Mali. The train only stopped in Bamako where they stayed for almost eight days.

According to Karamo, they left Bamako on a minivan for Burkina Faso where they stayed for five days sleeping in the streets like homeless people. Then they proceeded on the journey to Niamey, Niger from where they travelled across the desert to Libya. He told me it was the most dangerous journey he had ever embarked on. Karamo said the team he went with had no money on them to buy food and were only dependent on a female from another African country who was selling her body to buy food for the team. He said they had no choice but to rely on a woman despite knowing how she got the money. He told me if not for the woman the team would have died of hunger.

He said they became desperate when they reached Durko, where the team stayed for more than a week without money to buy food and drink. He said it was from Durko that they caught a truck to Tripoli, Libya. The journey to Tripoli, according him, lasted ten days during which some members of the team collapsed several times partly because the truck was overloaded with people to the point that getting ventilation was almost impossible and there was no water and food to consume. Karamo said they were disappointed that upon their arrival in Tripoli they were told by some Libyans that they were not welcomed. He said it did not take long before some of them began to receive slaps and other forms of maltreatment.

Karamo said an incident occurred that he would never forget and that was when one of their colleagues from the sub-region was beaten to death while they stood watching. According to him, those who did that accused the guy of only starring at a Libyan female that passed by them. He said immediately that was done they knew they were in the wrong place but that they preferred to face the difficulties than to return home. The struggle for survival, he said, continued with a series of beatings and all sorts of cruel treatment. He said the only job he got was cleaning that paid little but he had to do it. Despite doing that casual job with low pay, he was one time accused of committing a crime that he had no knowledge of and before he knew it he was kept in jail.

Karamo said it was after he was released from jail that he managed to convince some other colleagues to travel with him to Algeria where they thought things would be better. The journey from Libya to Algeria, he said, was also very difficult considering that they were transported by a small vehicle that was so small that they sat on one another. He said the vehicle never reached where they wanted and they eventually ended up in the bush where they stayed for more than a week planning how to get to Spain. He said while in that desperate situation one lady in their midst gave birth in the bush. For him, that was another sad and shocking moment of his life as there was no medical care available for the woman.

He said they left the bush after some days with the lactating mother and walked for a week before they reached the Morocco – Spain border. The team stayed at the border for about two months and made a several attempts to cross to Spain but were eventually arrested and deported to Algeria. In Algeria, Karamo said he met his fellow Gambian male and they decided to swim over to Spain. He said they strapped five bottles to their bodies but the first time they tried, they were caught and were sent back to the border. Karamo said that was another lucky moment for them as they were not killed or sent to jail. They made another attempt and were able to swim for hours before they were spotted by Spanish guards on patrol boats, who caught them and maltreated them severely before handing them to Moroccan coast guards.

He said the Moroccan coast guards released them after some time and again they forced their way into the bush where they wandered around without knowing which direction to follow. The journey in the bush took several months during which time they saw a lot of dead bodies. After living in that horrific situation where they only saw dead bodies, the team decided to make a U-turn back to Rabat to look for a boat that would take them to Spain. There they met a Gambian who offered them some assistance in terms of feeding but the man was unable to give them shelter. He said they lived in the streets of Rabat for nearly three weeks waiting for a boat trip to Spain. He said they finally got a small boat that took sixty of them on a journey that lasted more than two weeks before they reached the harbour in Spain. The journey, he said, was never pleasant because of the constant fear of being spotted by coast guards many of who were brutal on migrants. Luckily, they finally arrived in Spain but they spent the first night in the bush before they could find their way to one of the refugee camps. They stayed in that camps for almost two months without hearing anything like job opportunity. He said they knew it was not going to be easy considering their refugee status and lack of documents to support them in searching for a job. They lived like that for years before some of them had the chance to get papers in Spain that eventually enabled them do some casual jobs. Karamo said he decided to share his experience on the 'back -way' journey with his fellow young men and women back in Africa to make them understand that the 'back-way' journey was more painful than slavery. While he urged his fellow youth not to embark on 'back-way' journey, he called on the developed countries to promote economic and political stability in Africa so as to help young men and women of Africa to have their dignity in Africa.

Talking to the elderly made me know that Africa has never experienced this kind of exodus of young men and women in search of a better life. They told me that the youth strive at all cost to reach Europe and America through the 'back-way' journey despite the risk associated with the journey. Also, the International Organization for Migration (IOM) has reported that the number of people crossing to Italy by sea continues to increase daily. Because there is no appropriate solution to this, I think the European policymakers should shift their attention from reinforcing their naval forces in the Mediterranean Sea to conduct patrols, arrest and deport would-be migrants to formulating polices to curb economic and political instability in Africa. To Africans the move to reinforce naval forces is not the solution instead they want Europe to open up for Africans to get opportunities like better jobs and have access to basic human facilities knowing well that migrants contribute to economies of their host countries like their native countries.

In fact, as European lawmakers plan to deter would-be migrants, poor people in search of protection also makes similar plans to look for alternatives to cross the Mediterranean Sea to Italy. It is important to know that going 'back way' was no longer considered a foolish decision instead it was a move supported by many people who have a dream of making a better life in Europe and to help their families back home. The seriousness of the mass movement of people across political borders has reached a point that most young men and women keep their plans to go through 'back way' secret until they leave their home countries because they fear their relatives will be worried considering the information on the media about the efforts of the European Union in trying to stop people from crossing to Italy or Spain. Another fear actually has to do with their governments that embark on discouraging them from travelling through the 'back way' by arresting people.

Even though most African governments continue to tighten security around their borders to deter people moving through the 'back way' hundreds of thousands of young African men and women continue to risk their lives on the perilous journeys across the desert to Libya before attempting to cross the Mediterranean Sea because of desperation. It is important to note that social media is being used by youth to influence one another to embark on the dangerous journey. They are able to convince each other easily because of the high rate of unemployment and poverty affecting them daily. Many people find it hard to imagine how difficult it is always for them to put food on the table for their families not to talk about paying school fees for the children.

Poverty has reached a level where many parents can only provide one or two meals a day for their families. It is because of that difficult situation that most parents are forced to pull their sons and daughters out of school as early as when they are in their early teens and make them to work with them on their farms so as to produce harvest that can bring income for the family. You need to visit many families and see for yourself how some people live. The move will enable you to see situations where more than five people share a room in which there is no mattress and even bed sheet to sleep on. You will also see huts without a sufficient window that allows air to enter. Apart from living in terrible conditions in terms of poor shelter many poor people battle with daily feeding. No matter how hard the poor people work; their rewards are always nothing at the end as they cannot receive anything good from their hard work.

It will interest the reader to know that despite that fact an increasing number of Gambians are literate, there are few job opportunities. For almost 22 years of rule in the Second Republic, the government failed to help the youth by creating employment opportunities for them. The recruitment process contaminated with nepotism thus leaving highly skillful people unemployed because they had no relation or connection in the government. With all these difficulties people had no choice but to sacrifice their lives with the intention to get their families out of poverty. It is a fact that remittances from Europe and America are what keep the majority of the people living in The Gambia moving.

It is an open secret that the majority of homes with big satellite dishes, flat television screens, wonderful vehicles, children's bicycles and toys are either owned by someone living abroad or a family member abroad supporting others back home. In the same way, many people in possession of expensive mobile phones, iPods, laptops and other attractive accessories either received the items from someone abroad or got it from overseas. Also, many of the solid and beautiful houses are built by people living abroad or those who got their fortunes from abroad. The truth is that just having a relative in Europe or America makes someone important in society so long as they send remittances, as opposed to someone without a good home and where there is none of his/her relatives living abroad that sends remittances.

I have seen situations where families that were least respected later turned to be one of the most respected because their people in Europe and America keep sending remittances that transformed their lives for good. However small they may be, remittances have completely changed the way they were originally viewed in society. The new look on them has positively impacted on their lives as it gives them the confidence to move freely in the community without being disrespected. This development has inspired many poor families to sell their animals such as cow and sheep as well as personal accessories so as to help their children go to Europe or America with the hope of changing their lives for better.

Like other young men in The Gambia, I met Sarja Manneh, a native of Banjullinding in the Greater Banjul Area who told me he had a dream that one day he would get married to a pretty girl. He said he knew that getting a beautiful girl to marry is no longer a question of being a handsome boy; rather, it is a question of having enough money. Sarja told me he sat down to think how he could realize his dream. He said it took him several hours before finally making the decision that the only way for him to get more money to realize his dream is to embark on the 'back-way' journey through the Sahara desert to Libya before his intended destination of Europe.

Sarja said he had to move in order to fulfil his dreams of getting a beautiful girl to marry and to support his family. Despite that ambition, Sarja was only relying on the proceeds from the sale of watermelons that he grew on the only tiny family farmland. He said he knew that in their community, if you did not go to Europe, you would not even get a good woman to marry. He told me that almost all his colleagues in their village had already left through the 'back way' for the same reason. Immediately he said that, I remember the stories shared by other people in the same area concerning their desire to leave in search of a better life. I also looked around Banjullinding and was convinced by his point after seeing lots of new houses which I was told are owned by people in the diaspora. Truly, Banjullinding used to be called a hamlet in the 1970s during which there were only a few houses.

Sarja told me that almost all the impressive-looking houses in Banjullinding are as a result of remittances sent from Europe and America by the people from the village. He said such are the people many parents like to give their daughters to marry. He said the only way he could get a good wife is to be like those guys, which is why he had to leave. To confirm his story, I went around the community talking to people about the matter and the responses received made me believe Sarja was right. In fact, the finding made me understand there are more than what Sarja said. You need to get money to be respected, considered and even have attention at important village functions. You also need to have money before the community will view you as a hard-working and serious person that is committed to keeping a family. These are some of the conditions that forced young men and women to go on the perilous journey with the aim of making money to support themselves and their families.

As political leaders discuss measures to stop people using 'back-way' journey to Libya before attempting to reach Europe, I urge them to engage the developed countries to support the developing countries economically. Leaders need to know that it always takes a great sacrifice and thinking before the young men and women embark on the 'back-way' journey in search of greener pastures. It is sad to see how these young men and women sit in the open cargo of pick-up trucks, holding wooden sticks tied to the vehicle, as they move from Agadez in Niger to Libya.

A photo of would-be migrants in pick-up trucks

According to many of the young men and women who have returned from the 'back-way' journey, their initial horrific moment is always the moment when a pick-up truck loaded with migrants is driving against sandstorms in Agadez. The sandstorm, according to them, usually confuses the pick-up drivers, changes the topography, and even makes them lose direction. I also spoke with one national from a neighbouring country who told me some smugglers make the journey from Agadez with their pick-ups once every week carrying about 50 passengers. He said the only time the route looks good is when there is no sandstorm; smugglers carry lots of people across the Sahara Desert. The smugglers, according to him, usually do not care about their welfare; instead, they are only interested in making money paid as fares.

Some pick-up truck drivers, he said, know their way around the Sahara Desert like their homes but others just take the risk which was the reason they usually get lost. Once the driver gets lost, the next thing is that the vehicle runs out of fuel and then water. Once fuel and water get finished, people stay in the Sahara Desert suffering and this is usually the time people gradually die because of lack of food and water. He said even if someone survives without water there is the risk of being attacked by bandits, rival smugglers and even other traffickers looking for chance to seize vehicles in the desert. He told me when it comes to the desert journey no one is safe until one gets out of the danger zone.

Many migrants use the route from Niger where people engage in trafficking for various economic reasons. Just like many African countries, Niger according to some returnees from the 'back way' is another poor country where many people do not have good employment. It is unfortunate that despite the country's poor condition many would-be migrant in Europe go there and stay in that country for months while planning to cross the desert. They told me because Niger is a poor country they believe it would be hard, if not impossible, to control smuggling in Agadez, because the town has little business activities going on there. According to them, smuggling is a crucial financial sustenance for many ordinary people living there. They said a smuggler can make up to 4.5 million CFA (£4,985) in one trip across the Sahara. If a smuggler continues transporting without distraction he can make up to £250,000 in one year. Considering the financial benefit the smugglers will continue until when they no longer receive young men and women on the journey.

Young men and women that went through the 'back way' will also tell you the difficulties encountered while crossing the Sahara Desert. They said another terrible moment is when they arrive in Libya. In Libya, according to the returnees, most passengers are dropped off in Qatroun, the first major town over the border or in Sabha further to the north. They said because not all passengers usually pay their smugglers upfront due to lack of money, they are usually locked in various compounds referred to as illegal detention centres and remain there until their families or sympathetic fellow local migrant workers pay a ransom to the bandits to free them.

They said only those that paid smugglers in Niger where the journey began are allowed to go and find other smugglers to take them north through the desert to Tripoli, the capital of Libya. In case someone has no money he/she is, according to them, is usually forced to pick up any dirty job that would help him/her earn some money to be able to proceed on the journey. They told me because the majority usually remains in the hands of the smugglers, they are maltreated. They said the cruel treatment of migrants in Libya has completely turned the whole movement of people to human trafficking. Young men and women are mishandled and are usually subjected to all forms inhumane treatment while in the hands of what they referred to as "human traffickers" across the Sahara Desert. They said that the entire movement of the smugglers from Niger to Libya makes them believe the smugglers operate in networks. They said until these networks are destroyed smuggling across the Sahara Desert is not going to be stopped anytime soon.

After listening to the different stories, I believe that to curb the smuggling networks, there has to be economic and political stability in Africa. It is always important to know that most people who use the 'back-way' journey are young men and women that often carry with them children. These people are forced to risk their lives as they want to reach Europe where they are hopeful of earning good money that could support them and their families back in Africa after so much hardship in their native country. They have been suffering from violence and poverty that continue to prevail in their countries. They are in desperate need of economic well-being. This is not to say I support the movement of people across the desert but the fact is that people are leaving due to poverty, lack of protection and civil wars that continue to displace and take the lives of innocent people.

The move by the European Union to reinforce their naval forces in the Mediterranean Sea to curb the movement of people across the Mediterranean Sea has led to the use of dangerous means by the same people in order to reach Europe by all means. Because the migrants cannot cross the Mediterranean Sea by themselves, it has led to their inhumane treatment by bandits, criminals, and other cruel groups that pick and lock them in camps in Libya as reported by many returnees.

Many of the returnees I spoke with said Libya has lots of illegal detention centres where the bandits keep migrants demanding money from them. They said anyone that could not meet their demand was subjected to severe beating and other sorts of maltreatment. I felt sad when I first read in the media that the UNHCR tried to help refugees move out of the detention centres but could not due to little freedom accorded to the agency in Libya. The information made it clear that Libya is no longer a stable place since the fall of Muammar Gaddafi. The country has a problem to deal with because we all have seen in the media different groups fighting to control certain places. Nevertheless, because of violence and poverty that people continue to face they have no choice but to search for greener pastures elsewhere in the developed countries.

Anyway, with all the difficulties encountered on the 'back way' via Libya, many migrants mainly in Italy and Spain do not like to share their distressed circumstances for fear of being labelled as cowards, especially by their families that sacrificed their animals or other valuable to support their journeys. Instead of showing the true picture they use social media by putting photos that only make their peers back home believe they are in good conditions. Most people do not understand that the majority of migrants find beautiful places around them, take photos that they post on Facebook just to attract their loved ones back home in Africa. Most of the migrants were tormented, maltreated and almost enslaved in Libya by various groups of bandits according to many returnees. As the world gets more information about how migrants are maltreated in Libya by human traffickers there is a need to promote economic and political stability in Africa to help the people live in peace and prosperity. While Africans are not blaming the West for their failures, they want the developed countries to support Africa improve the continent's economic status so as to create employment opportunities for its people. Resources injected in buying weapons could be diverted to support institutions capable of training and hiring people. It is important to know that peace cannot prevail where there is hunger and starvation. I always cry each time there is news of migrants' boat capsize, killing hundreds of young men and women who only risked their lives in search of greener pasture. The future generation of African will be lost if immediate actions is not taken to protect the young men and women of the continent. The campaign against the 'back-way' journey should immediately be shifted from reinforcing the naval force in the Mediterranean Sea to providing entrepreneurship development programmes that could create employment opportunities in Africa.

3

The Mediterranean Sea Crossing and Loss of Lives

The Gambia like many African countries has experienced the worse brain drain and grief due to the mass exodus of young men and women through the 'back-way' journey across the Sahara Desert. The huge movement of the country's young generation has left towns, villages and hamlets virtually empty. The previous ghettos and football pitches have almost turned into zoos where you only find small animals roaming all through the day. The mass exodus through the 'back way' has not left behind some public servants, security personnel and even school children most of who left their education as they get inspired by remittances sent from their colleagues in the diaspora. Similarly, a good number of security personnel left the country in the Second Republic as they got discouraged with their pay cheque and constant threats on their lives by the autocratic government in place at the time.

While only a few of these people actually made it through the 'back way' to Europe, many people lost their lives in the desert and in the Mediterranean Sea. The great number of lives lost in the Mediterranean Sea, for example, has touched almost every family in the country. There were a number of people reported dead as their wooden or rubber boats capsized while attempting to cross the Mediterranean Sea. It was reported that the majority of these people usually boarded small boats that are usually over loaded to the point it was always difficult for anyone to move his/her legs. Someone who has experienced the journey told me that he joined a boat with lots of people and while they were sailing, the waves intensified and before they knew it all of them were already in the water. He told me he only saw himself under the boat struggling to hold the part of the boat. According to him, lots of other people were also shouting for help at the time when there was no helper. He told me as he managed to hold the boat before rescuers arrived; he saw dead bodies floating in the sea.

According to him some of these people wore lifejackets but despite that they died. He said they actually lived in the sea for some time before the Italian Coast Guards could reach them. While everyone was struggling, many of them got tired and eventually died in the sea. He told me there were women and children on the boat many of whom later died as well. He said the sad memory will live with him for many years as he keeps reflecting on the difficult moments of his life. However, with all the reports of increasing number of dead toll in the Mediterranean Sea poor people continue to be more committed to the 'back-way' journey because of the frustration of unemployment and insecurity in their home countries.

According to the Amnesty International, over two thousand five hundred people died attempting to reach Europe through 'back way' in just the first nine months of 2014. The majority of these people according to the report travelled from Eritrea, Syria, Afghanistan and Somalia crossing by boat from Libya to Italy and Malta. These people tried to cross the Mediterranean Sea on overloaded fishing boats that are naturally too small to carry the large number of people. A report published by UNHCR stated that in 2016 three thousand seven hundred and forty lives had lost just short of the three thousand seven hundred and seventy-one reported in the whole of the year 2015.

This was one of the worse experiences according to UHHCR spokesperson William Spindler during a press briefing in Geneva, Switzerland. According to him, the high loss of lives takes place despite a large overall fall in 2016 in the number of people seeking to cross the Mediterranean Sea to Europe. He stated that the likelihood of dying between Libya and Italy is even higher, at one death for every forty-seven arrivals while referring to what is called the Mediterranean route. He believed that the smugglers use lower-quality vessels-flimsy inflatable rafts that usually do not last the journey. Several incidents, according to Spindler, seem to be connected with travel during the bad weather. UNCHR however called on countries to do more to save lives.

Overcrowded migrant boat

While this is a sad story that affects lots of families around the developing countries, the European Union policymakers should make policies to help developing countries economically so that they can create employment opportunities for their people. It is always important to know that that people who risked their lives across the Mediterranean Sea to Europe had to leave their countries because of poverty, violence and intimidation. Besides the disaster in the Mediterranean Sea, some migrants said upon their arrivals in Europe they end up in camps in Italy and Spain where they stay for far too long without any employment opportunity.

Lamin Sonko a native of Jarra was among the few who were lucky to leave the camp in Italy for the Netherlands. He visited The Gambia after two years. I met him to discuss his experiences in Italy. Lamin said he one day sat on a chair near a playground in Ferrara, Northern Italy. After sitting and thinking for some time he got traumatized. He told me as a proud young boy he was totally embarrassed by the donated clothes he wore. According to him this was after a year when he was pulled from a stricken boat near the coast of Libya by the Migrant Offshore Aid Station. While narrating the story Lamin shed tears before telling me that he left his welding profession for Europe with the hope of fulfilling his dream of getting rich quickly. He told me it was his dream that forced him to experience difficult situations across the Sahara Desert and before another shocking disappointment in one of the camps in Italy.

Lamin said it all began when he like many others had the belief that they were grown men who must struggle to save their families from miserable poverty. He said it was however sad that many people who left with similar wishes did not realize their dreams. While many died during the journey, some ended up living in asylum camps where they got disappointed for not getting an employment that could help them support their families back home. When I asked to know if life was better for him in Europe, Lamin shook his head unhappily before telling me he did not achieve anything and could not tell if life would ever be better for him out there considering the kind of jobs he and other do for a living in the Netherlands.

According to Lamin, he was able to visit The Gambia following arrangements with a white lady that promised to join him in The Gambia for marriage. Despite taking the move to come and wait, Lamin said he was worried because not many people had succeeded getting back to Europe through such arrangements. Again when I asked why he took the decision in the first place, Lamin said he thought getting married to a native white lady from the Netherlands was the only way he could have a better life there. He said getting married could help him get papers that could assist in getting a better job. He added that getting married to a native could serve as security for him.

When I asked why he left The Gambia at the first place, Lamin said he left the country because his family was struggling with survival and as the breadwinner of the family his income from the welding profession at the time was too small to take care of him and his family. He told me there were many of them in the family and because of that a bag of rice lasted not more than a week. He said his family found it hard to pay the school fees for the school going boys and girls and they depended on his low earning that could not provide enough food let alone paying school fees. His parents, according to him, were old to the point they could no longer carry out physical work to support the family. He said it was because of the frustration and sympathy for his parents that he took the perilous 'back-way' journey before eventually seeing himself in the Netherlands.

Lamin said since he left The Gambia, his family had been relying on the remittances he sent monthly to buy rice, pay school fees and provide medical care. He told me it was unfortunate that most migrants live in camps where they were given little allowances part of which is what some people send back home to help their families. He told me many migrants living in camps spend their days in parks or loiter outside bus and train stations. They usually get homesick and shocked that with all the risk they took to reach Europe their new life offers few or no opportunities for them. Like many young men and women Lamin said he thought life in Europe is better than Africa but this was not the case as many of his colleagues in Italy and elsewhere continue to battle with survival. He said he knew a Gambian who was sleeping in a homeless shelter in Italy after being thrown out of his asylum lodge for reasons that were not communicated to him. He told me he cried after seeing that and what came to his mind was the fact that despite the young innocent guy going through hell he had the ambition to move on because his family back home have high expectations from him.

Though the dream of a better life does not usually come easy many of the migrants undergo lots of difficulties both on the 'back-way' journeys and during their stays in asylum camps as narrated by many migrants. Despite the horrific conditions, these people prefer to live and struggle in Europe because they know what awaits them if they decide to return home without money. This is the case considering the fact that the majority of these people sold either the only valuable asset like plot of land belonging to their family or small animals to reach Europe with the hope of getting more money to support their families. Because they have that fear of being abandoned or labelled as aimless when they return home without lots of money, they sacrifice to live in terrible situations in Europe. Also, it would be a difficult decision for the lots of young men and women that through the 'back way' to return home unsuccessful knowing very well that there are little or no employment opportunities back home. It is undeniable that lots of youth are unemployed despite having the basic academic qualifications and skills that could add value in national development. Because they cannot get employment many young men and women embark on the perilous 'back-way' journey with intention of reaching Europe where they could get employment to support their families.

It was because of the frustration that young men and women continue to embark on the 'back- way' journeys despite the heavy loss of lives in the Mediterranean Sea. In fact, there was a report by the Amnesty International that the year 2017 is the deadliest year for people trying to cross the Mediterranean Sea in desperate attempts to reach Europe. The Amnesty International report, called "A Perfect Storm: The Failure of European policies in the Central Mediterranean", associates the rising death toll in the sea, which has seen two thousand deaths since January 2017. The road between Libya and Italy according to the report has become the primary means for people arriving in Europe through the perilous journey.

It was reported that by giving non-governmental organizations the biggest share of responsibility for search and rescue in the sea crossing, Europe's governments have failed to prevent drownings and the terrible exploitations, including torture and rape that are faced by thousands of people in Libyan detention centres. The report also indicated that the European Union leaders histrionically reduced the number of deaths at sea in 2015 when they implemented measures to fortify search and rescue ability in the central Mediterranean, including providing more rescue boats closer to Libya territorial waters. The report has however indicated that governments then changed their approach, instead of stopping the departures of boats from Libya in order to keep the number of influxes in Europe down it focuses on strengthening coastguards for rescue mission. The Amnesty International described that as "a failing strategy that has led to ever more risky crossing and a threefold rise in the death-rate from 0.89% in the second half of 2015 to 2.7 & in 2017".

The report critiqued the European Union for "concentrating on strengthening the Libyan coastguard's capability to prevent departure and stop boats which often put people at risk rather than deploy an adequate resourced and dedicated humanitarian operation near Libyan territorial waters". The Amnesty International has been made aware of allegations that members of the Libyan coastguard have abused people, with some even shooting guns towards boats. A United Nations report published in June 2017 on the situation in Libya had similar findings. It has mentioned a number of human rights violations against people including "executions" torture and deprivation of food, water and access to sanitation. The report added that some well-known coastguards in Libya are directly involved in the sinking of people boats using firearms.

While these atrocities were committed in the Mediterranean Sea, families back home mourned the death of their loved ones. In fact, it got to a point that it was always a matter of time before another family receives news of their loved ones dead in the Mediterranean Sea. Almost all families in The Gambia are affected because the country is so small to the point that almost everyone is related. There were reports that some single families in the Gambia have lost more than three people in the Mediterranean Sea. They got traumatized and continued to mourn their deceased coupled with the fact that they had sold all their precious belongings to see their children reach Europe. There were other categories of families that do not know the whereabouts of their children for a couple of years now. These children were among the young men and women who left The Gambia in search of greener pastures.

As the desire to reach Europe continues through the 'back way' more and more people were reported dead in the Mediterranean Sea. It was reported that more than two thousand people died in the Mediterranean Sea in 2017 alone while on treacherous boats attempting to cross to Europe. This information was released on World Refuge Day, 2017. It was also reported by the UNHCR in 2017 that one hundred and twenty-nine Asylum seekers got missing and were assumed dead following a boat launched by smugglers in Libya started taking on water and eventually sank leaving only four survivors who are from sub-Saharan Africa. Two survivors told the International Organization for Migration that the boat had been at the sea for some hours when a group of Libyans believed to be "pirates" approached their boat using speedboat and forcefully took their motor. These survivors are reported to be in terrible state of shock by what they experienced according to the spokesman for International organization for Migration Flavio Di Giacomo who also stated that motor theft in the sea had led to numerous disasters.

It was also reported that a boat carrying about eighty-five people, including women and children mainly from Syria and North Africa sank in the Mediterranean Sea in 2017 while they attempted to cross to Europe. According to the UNHCR the disasters in the Mediterranean Sea were a recap of the severe dangers facing people that are forced to flee their countries by poverty, violence and maltreatment. While this is the fact an urgent action is needed to help desperate people from heinous and cruel treatment in the hands of smugglers. These people had already undergone a series of cruelty in their countries and because they had to leave they decided to embark on the perilous journey through the Mediterranean Sea in search of a better life. They deserve better treatment and should be accorded respect. It is disheartening to know that the poor people in search of protection and better life are maltreated by smugglers by beating them severely as they could not meet their demand for huge sums of money. The European Union and all international humanitarian agencies should do more to help migrants held by bandits and other criminals in Libya who held them in detention centres only to subject them all sort of inhumane treatment.

As the European Union stated that almost eighty-three thousand people that reached Europe in 2017 came by sea using the Mediterranean Sea between Libya and Italy, the route that is proven deadliest they should work out better modalities to accommodate these people by giving them employment instead of urging them to return to their home countries. What European Union should focus on is to find the root causes of this mass movement of people across the Mediterranean Sea. The move will help the EU know that these people left their countries due to violence, poverty and intimidation. It will then help the EU redirect it efforts to supporting economic and political stability in Africa by committing funds to build manufacturing companies that could create employment for the people.

Let the European Union also know that as the civil war in Libya continues following the removal of Muammar Gaddafi, bandits in Libya have set up ruthless trade with migrants trying to reach Europe through Libya by habitually capturing, asking for ransom, beating, raping and even selling migrants in "slave markets". These heinous acts are being reported by other people who were lucky to escape the inhumane treatment in the hands of the smugglers in Libya. They continue to tell their experiences in Libya while urging the international community to do more to help free vulnerable people, including women and children from the hands of many bandits in Libya.

In addition to the cruel treatment meted out on lots of people in Libya by the smugglers, the Human Rights Watch has also reported that the Libyan coastguards were engaged in reckless conduct during the operations to force the boats carrying people trying to Europe to return back to land in violation of international laws. Furthermore, the report highlighted incidents reported by The Independent in May 2017 that the coastguards opened fire while blocking recues by Non-Government Organization's ships in the international waters. It was indicated that the European Union made mistakes by entrusting the lives of people in need of rescue to Libyan coastguards. This is supported by a number of people who attempted to cross the Mediterranean Sea as they accused the Libyan coastguards of inhumane treatment on vulnerable people using boats to cross to Europe.

It is stated in the media that Italy which is housing more than one hundred and ninety thousand asylum seekers in state funded accommodation, has critiqued other European countries for failing to resettle asylum seekers and help rescue efforts. In a speech on World Refuge Day, the Italian Prime Minister Paolo Gentiloni said he was sorry that not everyone, including Europe, has shown the same willingness to take people in as done by Italy. He believed the refugee issues is a global phenomenon. The statement made by him was a fact because the movement of people across international borders has been going over thousands of years ago. People move for various reasons and unless concerted efforts are made to know the root causes to find solutions, the issue of repatriation will not work as it only increases frustration for poor and those in need of protection.

It was reported in the media that the Italian navy and coastguard alone rescued 41 per cent of the people trying to cross the Mediterranean Sea in 2016, Non-governmental Organizations ships 26 per cent, and ships from the European union-wide operation Sophia 25 per cent . In the first four months of 2017, the proportion of recues conducted by Non-governmental Organizations has increased to 35 per cent according to a new report while the Italian authorities carried out a third and operation Sophia carried out 16 per cent.

While some efforts are made by European countries such as Italy and Spain other countries have refused to accept refugees. It was the reason the European Commission opened a legal case against Poland, Hungary and the Czech Republic for refusing to take in asylum seekers under the 2015 plan to relocate migrants from Italy and Greece. The fact that these countries refused to take asylum seekers means the European Union has to do more in the area of making it members countries understand the need to help people who flee their countries due to violence, poverty and persecution. If the European Union succeeds in persuading its member states to accept asylum seekers it will reduce pressure in Italy and would enable the government of Italy to provide more support to the new arrivals. There should not be any move to intercept desperate people at sea and force them to return to Libya because they only end up in the hands of bandits who keep them in illegal detention centres and subject them to severe beating and rape.

As young men and women are dying in the Mediterranean Sea, the Nigerian Immigration Service said almost ten thousand Nigerians died between January and May 2017 while they attempted to cross to Europe. The NIS Assistant Comptroller-General, in charge of training, manpower and development, Mr Maroof Giwa, said that four thousand nine hundred Nigerians died in the Mediterranean Sea while the rest of the people died while going through the desert in their bid to reach Europe. This is very sad considering the fact that the people left their country with the intention to reach Europe where they could have better opportunities to help their families back home. These figures produced by Nigeria alone are a clear indication that the future generation of Africa is losing. Almost every country in Africa, particularly the West and North, have lost huge number of young men and women in the Mediterranean Sea. An urgent action is required to prevent the completed destruction of the future generations of Africa from disappearing in the Mediterranean Sea.

The International Organization for Migration (Switzerland) reported that forty-two thousand, nine hundred and seventy-four migrants and refuges entered in Europe in 2017. Over 80 per cent arrived in Italy and the rest in Spain and Greece. This compares with two hundred and five thousand, six hundred and thirteen through the 19 April 2016. To show the magnitude of the exodus by people as reported by International Organization for Migration (IOM) I have deemed it necessary to provide the table below showing arrivals by sea and deaths in the Mediterranean Sea from the year 2016 to 2017:

	January 1 to April 19, 2017		January 1 to April 19, 2016	
Country of arrival	**Arrivals**	**Deaths**	**Arrivals**	**Deaths**
Italy	36,703	898 Central Med. Route	25,353	83 Central Med. Route
Greece	4,761	14 Eastern Med. Route	179,585	376 Eastern Med. Route
Cyprus	Nill	-	27	
Spain	1,510	50 Western Med. Route	648	34 Western Med. Route
Estimated Total	**42,974**	**962**	**205,613**	**1,263**

Source International Organization for Migration

The spokesman for International organization for Migration said that thirty-six thousand, seven hundred and three migrants influxes to Italy by sea in 2017 exceeded by more than ten thousand, the number of arrivals at the same time during 2015 and 2016 respectively. He reported that over eight thousand, three hundred and sixty migrants have been rescued and brought to Italy since rescue operations were carried out on the high seas from 14 to 16 April 2017. He indicated that migrants had been travelling on 55 separate rubber boats, each carrying between 110 to 150 people, as well as at least three large wooden vessels, carrying 200, 250 and 500 people respectively.

The Ministry of the Interior of Italy has provided figures on countries that migrants come from to Europe between 2014 and 2015 as well as 2016 to end of 2017. It stated the following countries where migrants come from in 2014 and 2015: Eritrea, Nigeria, Somalia, Sudan, Syria and The Gambia. Arrivals by sea to Italy and countries of origin:

January to October 2014 and 2015			
No.	Countries of origin	2014	2015
1	Eritrea	32,537	37,796
2	Nigeria	6,951	19,576
3	Somalia	4,113	11,020
4	Sudan	2,370	8,692
5	Syria	32,681	7,232
6	The Gambia	6,179	6,759
	Total	**154,189**	**140,987**

Source: Italian Ministry of the Interior

Below is the breakdown of numbers of migrants that entered Italy according to Italian Ministry of the Interior and International Organization for Migration:

- It has indicated in 2014 alone a total of 170,100 migrants arrived in Italy.
- Arrivals by sea to Italy, 01 January to 26 November 2015 is 143,114*
- In October 2015, a total of 8,916 entered Italy. This information is provided by the Ministry of Interior, Italy.
- In November 2015, a total of 2,127 as reported by IOM as of 26 November 2015
- Main countries of origin according to the reports are: Eretria, Nigeria, Somalia, Sudan, Syria, Gambia, Mali, Senegal, Bangladesh and Ghana.

The main departures country as indicated in the report is Libya (while some departures are from Egypt, Greece and Turkey).

The table below contains arrivals by sea to Italy, January to October 2014 and 2015 respectively.

The report produced by Italian Ministry of Information also indicated that

	2014	2015
January	2,171	3,528
February	3,335	4,354
March	5,459	2,283
April	15,679	16,063
May	14,599	21,221
June	22,641	22,905
July	24,031	23,186
August	24,774	22,607
September	26,107	15,922
October	15,393	8,916
Total	154,189	140,987

Source: Italian Ministry of the Interior

countries of Guinea, Nigeria, Bangladesh, Ivory Coast, and The Gambia have each sent at least two thousand migrants through the first three months of 2017. The statistics are remarkable in the case of Bangladesh which recorded just a single arrival by sea from Africa during the first three months of 2016, compare with two thousand eight hundred and thirty one in 2017. The table below indicates the comparison of arrivals for migrants to Europe in March 2017 and March 2016. It also includes their countries of origin.

Countries of Origin	March 2017	March 2016
Gambia	2232	2270
Guinea	3168	1594
Nigeria	3159	3415
Ivory Coast	2527	1541
Bangladesh	2831	1
Senegal	1915	1661
Morocco	1739	822
Mali	1141	1442
Somalia	634	1504
Eretria	577	615
Total	**24,292**	**18,777**

Source: Italian Ministry of the Interior

The Libya's Directorate for Combating Illegal Migration reported that Libyan fishermen sometime in 2017 found the bodies of 28 people in a boat off the cost of Subratah. This was reported by Christine Petre of the International Organization for Migration in Libya. She also stated that four thousand one hundred and twenty-nine people have been rescued off the Libyan coast with remains of two hundred and five migrants recovered.

The Worldwide IOM missing project reported that there have been one thousand four and eighty six mortalities through 19 April 2017, with the Mediterranean region accounting for the biggest quantity of deaths over half of the global total. This arises to seven hundred and thirty four less mortality than were reported up to the same time in 2016. Nonetheless, these data do not account for full reporting from North Africa and the Horn of Africa, two migration corridors where data collection seems to be slower than in other regions. It is sad that lots of people died while attempting to cross to Europe in search of a better life. The world needs to act quickly to prevent more human calamities in the Mediterranean Sea. This is possible when the developed world provides economic and political support to Third World countries thereby promoting the maintenance of peace, economic prosperity and stability. The move will undoubtedly reduce the influx of people moving to Europe in the name of looking for a better life.

No doubt crossing the Mediterranean Sea to Europe is so far the deadliest journey for people wishing to seek greener pastures in Europe. The United Nations has reported that at least 33, 761 have reported to have died or gone missing between the year 2000 and 2017. The report which was released by the International Organization for Migration stated the highest number of fatalities at 5,096, was recorded in 2016, when the short and relatively less unsafe route from Turkey to Greece was shut, following the European Union-Turkey deal. What the European Union failed to understand at the time was the fact that shutting the shorter and less dangerous routes leads to the opening of longer and more dangerous routes thus increasing the number of people dying at sea, according to Professor Phillippe Fargues of the European University Institute.

The reports released by the IOM examine available proof on trans-Mediterranean irregular migration to Europe along several routes going back to the 1970s, particularly on the magnitude of the flows, the evolution of sea routes to Southern Europe, the characteristics of migrants, the extent to which one can separate between economic and forced movements, mortality during the sea journey. Over 2.5 million migrants have crossed the Mediterranean Sea in an unauthorized fashion since the 1970s. It indicated that irregular sea journeys started rising in those years in response to the introduction by Western States grappling with rising levels of unemployment during the 1973 oil crises, of visa requirements for people who until then had been exempted - most of them temporary labour migrants from North Africa and Turkey. Those policies encouraged those who were already in Europe to stay, increased irregular migration of family members to join their relatives in Europe and gave way to the smuggling business, indicated by the report. It also highlights differences between the modern pattern of migration from Africa to Italy, mostly via Libya and that from the Middle East to Greece via Turkey.

It is important to note that arrivals to Italy from North Africa largely originates across sub-Sahara Africa in response to deep migratory pressures - population growth coupled with limited livelihood opportunities, high unemployment and poor governance and political and economic instability. People mainly from Africa risk their lives to Europe because they are looking for stability. It is a fact in developed world, especially the United States and United Kingdom, everything is stable: light, government, jobs and liberty. Evidently, People in those countries do not worry about losing their families, homes, money and businesses as a result of internal conflicts or military coups. People also move to get standard of living and value for their dignity. Seriously, when it comes to standard of living and value for human dignity Africa is 100,000,000 miles behind the developed world as evidenced in our daily life. People get arrested for just expressing their views and democratic rights. The get beaten and undergo all sorts of inhumane treatment for speaking against their governments. There are several instances where people get arrested and tortured for just supporting the programmes of an opposition political party.

People also leave Africa to look for job opportunities in the developed world because they cannot find a better life at home. It is a fact that getting an employment in most African countries is not an easy thing. In fact even after getting a job one finds it hard to take care of one's feeding and bills due to a very low pay. Trust me; some people take up certain jobs out of frustration because they have to support their families by buying a bag of rice monthly. Alongside the challenges of taking care of oneself with the low pay one also has to provide feeding and shelter for the extended family many of whom are usually jobless. In many households of more than 10, you find only one person doing a white-colour job. It is this person who provides feeding, settles medical bills, pay school fees for the children and ensure everyone in the family has a better shelter. Despite the low pay the person will have to support all these people once he/she is working or faces constant humiliation by the family members. Because not everyone can live with constant pressures some usually quit their jobs and embark on dangerous journeys through the 'back way' to Europe in search of better opportunities so as to help their families back in Africa.

The world needs to know that people in need of protection will continue to leave Africa and other parts of the less developed world in record numbers until their governments can implement policies that actually reduce poverty, violence, insecurity, tackle corruption, and reinforce weak institutions. As this is yet to be done, the developed world must accommodate and treat migrants with dignity as they search for protection. Also, the developed world should work closely with the Third World countries in addressing the already identified root causes of migration. Sending back migrants, including women and children only sends a message that people face inhumane treatment by the developed world that preaches respect for human rights and dignity. The developed world needs to know that when it sends people back they end up having nowhere to turn to for protection.

Many victims of violence, extortion, sexual abuses, and death threats do not get protection from their governments which were the reason they fled in search of safety. In fact many victims previously feared the police and other law enforcement agents in most developing countries than they feared criminals because instead of protecting them the police make their situations worse. In most African countries, the rule of law and law enforcement institutions are weak and corrupt. The majority of police forces and other law enforcement agents are underpaid, plagued by poor leadership, and sometime complicit in criminal activities. Most corrupt law enforcement agents use their low earnings as a cover to engage in unethical behaviours.

In The Gambia for example, there were growing concerns of the military and the former National Intelligence Agency (NIA) involvement in torture, extrajudicial killings and human rights abuses that were seriously troubling during the dictatorial rule. These mischievous acts forced many people to flee the country in search of a better life and protection elsewhere. Because of the bad treatment of innocent people they took the difficult decision to leave their countries. People need to know that the decision to migrate is a very complicated one, and a variety of factors, especially economic insecurity and family situation but the inhumane treatment of people by those who are supposed to protect them forced innocent people to relocate in search of protection. Truly, violence and insecurity are major drivers for the growing number of Africans leaving their countries through the 'back-way' journeys across the desert in the name of searching protection mainly in the developed countries where there is political and economic stability.

The world needs to know that the poor economic condition and civil wars that forced people to go to Europe and elsewhere in the developed countries in search of greener pastures has got to a point where some married spouses got separated unceremoniously as husbands and wives abandon their partners and go through the 'back way'. The mass exodus through the 'back way' has also left many parents search their children before they could receive information about their presence in Agadez and Libya. It is a fact that many young men and women left through the 'back way' without letting their parents know about their movement. Most of these people left with only little money that they got either from the sale of some family properties without family consultation or precious personal belongings of their parents, particularly their mothers. There were reports of many young guys that took the belongings of their parents, sold them and left without informing people close to them. In fact there were several instances reported where some young men and women were sent to receive some remittances on behalf of their families and instead of bringing the money home they decided to embark on the perilous 'back-way' journey with the remittances.

One Mamadou Sonko, a native of Serekunda in the Greater Banjul Area, told me he woke up one fateful morning and walked to the boys' quarters in his compound usual to check on his brothers and nephew before leaving for work. According to him, he was surprised that day; he did not meet his nephew in the house. He said when he asked about the reason he was not in the house at the time he got the response that his nephew did not sleep in the house. Mamadou said he could not understand that considering the fact that he always knew when each of the boys was to travel. He said he stood at the door for some time asking many questions but there was no response about his nephew's whereabouts.

He told me he left for work thinking what could have happened that forced his nephew to spend night outside the house without him knowing. He got to work and only returned in the evening and asked if there was any information about his nephew and nobody said they got news about him. Mamadou said after having lunch he decided to go out and was luck to meet a friend that he shared the story with as he was worried. He said it was his friend who advised him to calm down as he was reminded that many young men and women were moving through the 'back way' as they got influenced by their colleagues who were in Agadez and Libya. Mamadou said while he initially found it difficult to be convinced he later asked himself to wait for any news of such movement of his nephew. According to him, it was after a couple of days that he received international call that it took him several seconds before receiving because he did not know the number, especially the country code.

Mamadou said when he finally received the call it was his nephew. He said when he asked about his location his nephew told him he was in Agadez, Niger but needed some money to continue on the journey across the desert. He told me his response to his nephew was that he could not understand the reason he left in the first place but the discussion according to him seemed not interesting to his nephew because he was only interested in getting money as he said his life was threatened. His nephew even told him that if he failed to help he could lose his life. He said like many parents who were put in worried situation, he had no choice than to quickly find money and send to him. He said he thanked God that he was able to send some money after two days. The next time his nephew called according to Mamadou was to inform him that he received the money and was going to leave for Saaba before getting to Tripoli, Libya. Mamadou said, to his dismay, his nephew instead of saying thank you to him asked for more money to enable him to pay boat to cross the Mediterranean Sea to Europe upon arrival in Tripoli.

He said it was another shocking moment for him because he had no money left. According to him, he had to go and borrow money to send it to him because he feared that his nephew could be adopted by bandits in Libya as there were reports of migrants being held in illegal camps. He told me it was after he sent the money that his nephew paid the boat that took them to Europe across the Mediterranean Sea. He told me he only realized that many parents experienced similar things after speaking with many in society. Mamadou said he could not still understand the reason his nephew left because he got all the support at home. When he finished I told him people left through the 'back way' for various reasons not just economic and that he needed to find out from others and free himself from regretting what he knew nothing about.

Also, in my neighbourhood in Tallinding in the Greater Banjul Area, one mother has reported her young boy missing after taking her ipad cell phone that worth around twenty-five thousand three hundred dalasiS (US$550). As people stood with her searching for the boy, she got information after four days from her son who told her that he had sold the ipad phone and the money was used to pay for the route to Agadez, Niger. According the woman, instead of her son asking for forgiveness he requested for additional financial support to enable him to pay traffickers in Agadez so as to be transported across the desert to Libya. She said because she loves her son so much she had no choice than to sell her only precious jewelry and send the proceeds to the boy in Agadez. She said she has sent money to her son on three occasions before the boy could reach Italy. Like her many other parents, particularly mothers, have done similar things for their children most of who left without letting them know their plans. The 'back way' movement has forced parents to provide financial support to their children because they feared their children might get into trouble if they were left without money on foreign land. Seriously, many parents really suffered in terms of getting monies to send to their children on the 'back-way' journeys. This is the reason I find it very sad to see some of those children returning without money.

Let people know that the world is today more connected than ever before and social media plays an important role by disseminating information. It is a fact that many people who left through the 'back way' got information about the route to Agadez from their colleagues on social media. Because they lived a life that is difficult they were easily convinced to move in search of a better life. These people need support, protection and it is the reason they should be accommodated to enable them to live in dignity. Like information, commodities and money flow rapidly across national and international boundaries, a phenomenon referred to as globalization so human beings who are looking for protection should be allowed to move freely. Interestingly, while industrialized countries are supporting easier flows of money, goods and services, they are at the same time restricting the movement of people. The Third World countries view this as double standard, especially since labour is an important factor in the production of goods and services.

The Global Commission on International Migration (GCIM) stated that between 1960 and 2000, the share of merchandise exports and trade in service has roughly doubled, owing to new global trade policies negotiated at the World Trade Organization (WTO). But during the same period the share of international migrants in relation to the world's population has increased only slightly, from 2.5 to 3 percent. This according to the report was due to increasing restriction on official migration, which is also partly to blame for the rise in illegal migration.

The report stated that by 2000 there were an estimated 175 million migrants worldwide, most moving from low–to-higher-income nations. About 9 percent -163 million-were Africans, down from 12 percent in 1960. Between 5 and 12 percent of the population of 30 industrialized nations are migrants.

The former United Nations Secretary General Kofi Annan once said migration brings with it "many complex challenges". The issues according to him include human rights, economic opportunity, labour shortages and unemployment, the brain drain, multiculturalism and integration, and a flow of refugees and asylum seekers. Policy makers according to him must grapple with issues of law enforcement. He said the world cannot ignore the real policy difficulties posed by migration, "but neither should the world lose sight of its immense potential to benefit migrants, the countries they leave and those to which they migrate".

Mr Annan said owing in part to labour shortages in certain sectors, an expanding global economy and the long-term trend of ageing populations, many industrialized countries need migrants. They face shortages in highly skilled areas such as information technology and health services, as well as in manual jobs in agriculture, manufacturing and construction. Many turn a blind eye to irregular migration to fill jobs locals do not want to take on, he said.

This statement made by former UN secretary General is accurate and reflects the realities involving migration. The developed world needs to know that the developing countries are demanding more open policies towards migration. They consider migration as offering an opportunity to reduce the ranks of the unemployed, earn revenue through the remittance of workers' earnings, and imports skills, knowledge and technology via returning residents. Despite this, the developing countries are also concerned about the losing skilled workers to developed countries, a process referred to as the brain drain.

It is a fact that most people who seek to migrate are forced by terrible circumstances in their home countries such as poverty, civil war, torture, persecution, rape and other sexual abuses. In most emigrants-producing countries, jobs are scarce and salaries are too low to help workers sustain themselves and support their families. These are the compelling factors that forced people to leave their countries to search a better life somewhere in the developed world.

The ILO Director General Juan Somavia once said that globalization has not so far led to the creation of sufficient and sustainable decent work opportunities around the world. He said so far "better jobs and income for the world's workers has not been a priority in policy-making". It is a fact that many African countries have failed to create jobs, despite pursuing structural adjustment policies recommended by the World Bank and the International Monetary Fund. What is happening is that there has been a decline in job opportunities and real income in many African countries. It stated that between 1994 and

2004, the number of workers living on less than a dollar a day increased by 28 million in sub-Saharan Africa.

The UN Special Representative for West Africa Ahmedou Ould-Abdallah once said he dreaded to think of the scenes we may be contemplating in, say 20 years if we do not make a massive consolidated effort to create jobs and opportunities in West Africa. According to him "what is happening now is only a tip of the iceberg, compared to what will occur if urgent solutions are not found".

The Addis Ababa-based UN Economic Commission for Africa proposes that job creation policies on the continent focus on labour-intensive sectors such as agriculture. Governments according to ECA, Economic Report on Africa 2005 should work to minimize regulations to private, domestic and foreign investment, provide infrastructure and promote political systems that allows the majority of citizens to become involved. It indicated that recently, jobs being created in agriculture are in the informal economy, at low levels of productivity. These cannot provide workers with enough income to pull themselves or their families out of poverty.

Mr Philip Martin, a professor at the University of California in US once said even investment policies in industrialized nations, which could be used to manage the flow of migrants, are failing short. "The incentive to invest in developing countries is driven by expected profits, not the need for jobs to reduce emigrations". Mr Somavia also stated that "we don't need more diagnosing or one-size-fits-all solutions". He said it is time for the international financial institutions, the entire UN system and bilateral cooperation to focus energies on job creation in Africa, which according to him is fundamental to peace, security and unity.

The developed world needs to know that freer migration would be a quick means of increasing Africans benefit from globalization. The challenge is to develop policies that are acceptable to both the developed world and developing countries and that will undoubtedly outgrowth global economic growth. A former French President Jacques Chirac said during the France-Africa Summit in Mali in December 2016 that "together, Africans and Europeans have a duty to dismantle the illegal migration networks, behind which according to him include an appalling and mafia-like traffic". He also said that "together Africans and Europeans must encourage co-development and enable Africans to enjoy decent conditions for living and working in their own".

Like most parts of Africa, people leave The Gambia in search of better life elsewhere. These people are forced to leave due to poverty, unequal access to basic services such as good food, drinking water, shelter and even good health system. Many youth left at the time a dictator that was known for his human right abuses was ruing The Gambia. At the time, the situation of human rights activists, politicians and journalists was dangerous. The desperation of the people got to a point where there was a report of a series of abortive coup attempts where many brave soldiers were reportedly tortured and imprisoned on hard conditions. In fact, the populace saw them chained like slaves.

Beside the poor economic situation that affected lots of people at the time, many were forced to leave due to lack of protection from the government. The dictator at the time refused to promote democracy as a result the country saw governance failures that seriously impacted the whole country at the political and economic level. There was rampant unemployment and skyrocketing of prices that poor people could not afford. The government turned a blind eye to the plight of the poor but the leadership made sure that people were forced to support his doctrine or are dealt with inhumanely. This was the reason many people got problems for supporting opposition political parties.

It is a fact to say that many people in The Gambia got maltreated in the hands of some security agents, particularly the former National Intelligence Agency and soldiers during the Second Republic as revealed by former Junglers. There are lots of people that continue to tell other people how they were tortured for only making their opinions known on how the country should be governed. One Lamin Ceesay, a native of Abuko in the Greater Banjul Area who was among the people that got pardoned by the government of President Barrow, told me he was electrically shocked in detention to the point that his arm was broken. According to him, the security agents hit him with a gun on his forehead to the point he nearly lost consciousness.

Apart from Lamin, I spoke with lots of the former prisoners released by the new government. They shared their bitter experiences by disclosing how they got maltreated in the hands of some bad security agents at the time. They told me the country had some wicked people in uniform who were only interested in saving the former president. These people said they were handled like animals and were given poor food. In fact, some told me that their inhumane treatment got to a point where a prisoner had to use pot as toilet and carry it when it was full. This according to them affected all irrespective of the status some of them had in society. Serious conditions like those and many others make Africans insecure in their countries.

Unfortunately, as the poor and vulnerable Africans are suffering, southern Europe is complaining of sensing the pressure of growing irregular migration flows from North Africa. As extraditions from Greece and other European countries come into full effect under the European Union–Turkey deal and smuggling networks from Turkey begin to weaken, Italy is also raising alarm for seeing a surge of arrivals by sea. It was reported on social media that the

Italian Prime Minister Renzi's recent" Migration Compact" aimed to adopt a similar mechanisms to control undocumented African migration to their shores by signing deals with Third World countries on the African continent. Renzi's proposal disregards initiatives that have already attempted this method - the Valetta Summit's 1.8 billion Emergency Trust Fund for Africa, for example. Rather than creating new and expensive ways to tackle irregular migration, creating incoherence in terms of policy goals as well as being highly inefficient, efforts should be put in place to improve those already prevailing.

Also, instead of tightening borders to prevent migrants entering Europe; efforts should be directed at making policy for the protection of vulnerable migrants. The European Union needs to understand that by tightening border controls, migration pattern shifted towards more dangerous routes. History enables me to know that until the year 2010, Gambians on the way to Europe travelled via Senegal coastal towns such as Kayar and Joal -Fadiouth, hoping to board pirogues (wooden boats) to the Canary Islands. Nonetheless, after a bilateral agreement was signed between Spain and Senegal, Frontex amplified its border patrols on the Western Mediterranean, acting as a strong deterrent for Gambians. Since then, the 'back-way' journeys have become the alternative route for people aiming to reach Europe in search of a better life.

The developed countries needs to know that any attempt to block migrants through increasing border controls or development hand-outs to corrupt countries with dubious human rights records will not prevent vulnerable and poor people from fleeing their countries in search of a better life. Also, the poor and vulnerable people should be handled with dignity after they manage to enter Europe following hardship on the 'back-way' journey, including torture, rape and intimidation in Libya as reported by many returnees. Furthermore, the developed countries need to know that by rejecting asylum applications on the basis of migrants' nationality or rapid filtering of migrants in the preidentification process in European Union "hotspot" system is equal to denying vulnerable people their basic and fundamental human rights to asylum.

In order to understand the kind of pain encountered by many poor young men and women of Africa, you need to speak to someone who had gone through the 'back way' to Libya and returned unsuccessfully. As more and more flights are bringing returnees from Libya, I made efforts to speak with many of them who shared their bitter memories of the dangerous journeys. One Sulayman Camara told me he was happy to have returned home while sitting on a bench outside his family house at Farato. He said to me, a few days ago he was languishing in a prison cell near Tripoli, his fourth spell in detention during his ten months in Libya, while trying to cross the Mediterranean Sea by boat to Europe.

According to Sulayman, his parents sold the only piece of land belonging to the family and paid his way out of his fourth stints in detention as well as the smuggling fee for him and another relative he met on the journey to enable them to take a boat to Italy. According to him, they were pickpocketed by street gangs and because all their money was taken away they could not proceed on their journey instead they landed back in one of the vicious detention camps that had sprung up all over ungovernable Libya and are used to extort ever greater sums from vulnerable migrants trying to cross the Mediterranean Sea to reach Italy or Spain.

"To be in prison in Libya was like fire," Sulayman told me while he looked frustrated. He told me he was beaten and saw lots of dead bodies in the detention centre. According to him, he was standing when his friend was shot dead because he attempted to escape. Sulayman said while living in constant fear of death, the International Organization for Migration visited them and gave them the choice of either to stay in that horrible condition or to return to The Gambia. According to him, he quickly chose coming back home because of the constant pain people go through in the hands of bandits in Libya. He said he did not want to stay in Libya anymore after all that he saw and went through in hands of cruel gangs. Sulayman said it was sad that black people are treated in Libya like slaves

Unfortunately, with all these pains encountered by young men and women from Africa, some African leaders still act defensive. It was sad that while the vulnerable young men and women left The Gambia, mainly during dictatorial rule, where they faced a series of inhumane treatment and poverty, the leader who held onto power for twenty-two years, constantly said those leaving the country at the time were unpatriotic. He refused to accept that the poor and vulnerable young men and women risk their lives by fleeing the country due to poverty, high level of unemployment and autocratic rule that only recognized those who danced to the tune of the leadership. The situation was difficult that even people who left through the 'back way' and did not find what they were looking for in Europe and elsewhere were reluctant to return home for the fear of inhumane treatment in the hands of some security agents working for the government at the time.

Thanks to God that The Gambia has gone through a successful change of government. The new coalition government has made tackling migration a priority. It plans to focus on creating jobs and training opportunities to reduce the high level of unemployment rate among the youth. No doubt when the new government succeeds in this it will drastically reduce migration as young people will get employed. The move will place the country in a better position when it comes to the issue of Gambians leaving their homes in search of a better life.

According to UNICEF, which analyzed Italian immigration data, nearly 0.5 percent of The Gambia's population migrates every year. The Gambia was also previously ranked highest among sub-Saharan Africa countries in terms of the numbers of its migrants who are unaccompanied minors. In 2016, 13 percent of unaccompanied children arriving in Italy were Gambians, according to UNICEF. In total, nearly 12,000 Gambians arrived in Italy via the Mediterranean in 2016, a 36 percent increase from 2015.

Considering the huge movements of people it should be clear that the 'backway' trend is only going to be addressed if there is economic and political stability in Africa. Honestly, re-enforcing the naval forces in the Mediterranean Sea, building more walls, tightening visa regimes and other means to restrict the movements of people are not the solutions to migration. People need to know that migration is a long phenomenon in the world. If by applying measures mentioned above would deter the movement of migrants, there was not going to be so many deaths. Not only is the world seeing the major force displacement of people in recorded history but also the largest spread of anti-immigrant sentiment seen in decades. The world needs to act urgently to address the issue of innocent people dying in the Mediterranean before it is too late to prevent the loss of generations in the sea.

It is interesting to hear that when migrants arrive in Malta or Lampedusa they go through proceeding centres. The question many migrants asked is why people would take the risk of putting their lives in danger if they could be processed before. They believe the ideal would be to have migrant processing centres on shore in North Africa, before they embark on the dangerous journey using boats to cross the Mediterranean Sea. They believe that when the world studies their conditions it will come to light that some migrants are qualified for refuge protection under the 1951 Convention while some are clearly economic migrants as indicated by evidence in many reasons given by migrants. Why can't the European Union advocate provision of opportunities for migrants or even short-term protection for them instead of thinking about returning them to their countries where they forced to flee as a result of poverty, intimidation and persecution?

4

Migrants' Contributions to Host and Sending Countries

Africa Migrants contribute to the economies of the host and sending countries by paying taxes to host governments and sending remittances to their home countries. This applies to all categories of migrants irrespective of the job they do. Despite the fact that most migrants take up casual jobs that the natives are usually in short demand, they pay taxes thus contributing to the Gross Domestic Product (GDP) of their host countries. As long as migrants continue to pay taxes the firms they work always get recognition from their host countries. I strongly believe no economies, both the developed and developing countries, can grow steadily in the absence of migrants' contribution. This is because of the pivotal role migrants play in contributing to the promotion of economies of their host and sending countries. They should be viewed positively and accorded respect at all times.

Has the developed countries forgotten that migration has been historically positive? Migrants bring new ideas and high motivation to the receiving countries. They contribute to the economies of their host countries more than to the economies of their countries of origin that they send remittances to support their families. Migrants take jobs that native usually don't like to do and work tirelessly despite earning little money. No matter how small the pay might be, migrants pay taxes thus contributing to the economies of their host countries. Most migrants would tell you that they are left with almost nothing after paying taxes to their host countries. It is sad that the good part of migrants' earnings goes back to the economies of their host countries. Sadly, it is that small left over that is sent to their native home countries where it is always highly needed to put food on the table for many people, pay school fees, provide medical care and foot electricity bills.

Because migrants contribute positively to the growth of the economies of their host countries they should be seen as an integral part of development in their host countries. It is the reason the developing countries cannot appreciate any move to label migrants bad knowing very well the kind of jobs they do in the developed countries from which they contribute to the economies of their host countries by paying taxes from the physical/casual jobs they do for a living. While there are some such debate on migrants issues, people need to know that the reasons for migration differs. Some people migrate due to troubles in their home countries such as civil war, floods or famine, poverty and insecurity while others leave due to intimidation and disregard of their basic human rights such as the right of free expression and political belonging. Other people take into consideration the environmental and economic benefits they can get in another place of living. Also, political and cultural reasons are on the list of those which drive people away from their homes. You need to know all this to be able to respect migrants and accord them the opportunity to work and earn a living in stable economic and political conditions. It is true that almost all migrants from Africa and some part of the Middle East fall under the mentioned reasons. They leave their countries in search of good life because there are so many troubles in their native countries.

It is important to realize that migration brings substantial benefits, by offering real advantages and rewards. Migrants exercise significant influence on the host countries. In case of labour shortage due to aging population, newcomers fill the open job vacancies. It happens that there are certain skill gaps; then the services of the experts from other countries can be beneficial for both sides. Experienced doctors or other highly skilled specialists are always in great demand. Construction workers, welders or other manual workers are never thrown idle, either. There are certain jobs which the natives are always unwilling to take, like those of babysitters, cleaning and maids working with aged people so such jobs are taken by migrants. Migrant workers pay taxes and fill the pension gap in the host country. Besides, new people always bring innovations, change and development, transforming the obsolete long-established approaches. Thus, migration can help the economic growth to be sustained. Moreover, it results in cultural diversity that makes a sustainable contribution to the history of the host country. Migration even has a potential of uniting people of different cultural backgrounds as they interact on a daily basis either at workplaces or schools, in some instances.

Also, some people move so as to get some advantages for themselves in terms of self-development. They move to improve their standards of living by getting better jobs, career advancement and increased the economic opportunities for themselves and their families back home. Whatever the migrants fall under they should be given the necessary protection. Many of the migrants in recent times flee from conflicts, persecution and poverty and because they left their countries to look for security and economic well-being, they should be accorded dignity. These people took risky journeys because they are forced to leave home due to a poor state of living. They only need a better life, health care system, education as well as other basic human needs for themselves and their children.

It is also important to know that some people left their countries because they experienced culture shock. While in Europe they get into contact with different people, gain new knowledge and skills and have better view of the world. When these people return to their countries they are usually among the most in-demand workers because of their advanced skills. If they are established, they are mostly happy in their destination, reaping gains in the form of better access to education and health, higher incomes and better prospects for themselves and future generations.

No doubt migration is advantageous to the host countries, the migrants and the sending countries, especially if it is legal and economically beneficial for both sides. It is the reason the rights for immigrants are to be fully protected at all times. They need to be treated with dignity and respect just like the locals or natives. To confirm this point I deem it important to state the comments made by Ms Laura Thompson, Deputy Director General, International Organization for Migration who made a speech in Brussels about the benefit migration brings to countries of origin and host as well as to migrants. The full text reads:

It is my pleasure to be here today in Brussels to talk about some of the opportunities and benefits that migration brings to countries of origin and destination as well as to the migrants themselves.

The XXI Century is the century of human mobility and migration. We can no longer think about our economies, societies or cultures without thinking about human mobility. According to all the available information, this human mobility is expected to increase and nearly double in the near future.

The arguments in favour of the facilitation of human mobility are not only human rights-based, but also demographic, social and economic. No one puts in question anymore the impact that aging populations, low birth rates, longer life expectancy and urbanization have in the economies and social protection systems of developed and high-middle income countries. The links between migration and development of countries of origin and destination are also much better understood and recognized today, and States are adopting policies and systems that enhance the positive impact of migration into their development and economic growth planning.

Despite the general acceptance that migration is inevitable, necessary and desirable, there is a worrying rise in discrimination, xenophobia, exclusion, and human rights violations of migrants throughout the world. The general public has predominantly negative feelings about migration and migrants, and a sense that governments do not have matters properly under control. This public perception has restricted the ability of politicians to advance the economic arguments in their discourse about migration and develop more realistic and fact-based policy and legislative frameworks.

That is why, I wish to challenge today some of the current misrepresentations about migration and the distorted way in which migration issues are discussed. I strongly believe that we need a more balanced evidence-based debate about migration, where the real facts are presented and discussed openly.

Let me begin by giving you a few examples.

First, a common misperception is that there are too many immigrants. Misconceptions so distort reality that in some European countries ordinary citizens estimates the number of immigrants at three times more than there really are. The 2014 Transatlantic Trends survey conducted by the German Marshall Fund showed that misinformation about basic migration facts is a key factor responsible for anti-immigrant sentiment. In countries like the United States, the United Kingdom, Greece, Italy and others, the proportion of people who agreed that there are too many immigrants in their countries fell sharply when people were told how many foreigners actually reside there.

A second misperception is that the majority of migrants come from the poorest parts of the world. in fact, the 2013 International Organization for Migration (IOM) World Migration Report shows that only about 40 percent of all migrants move from the global South to the global North. Over a fifth of migrants move across developed countries. People are just as likely to move between countries in the South as they are to move from South North.

Third, migration is commonly perceived as solely an immigration issue. How many European are aware that the British diaspora, some 5 million people, is the eighth largest in the World? we need to change our mind-set, especially given that a growing number of people are moving from the North to the South in search of work. you are all familiar with examples of Portuguese moving to Angola or Spanish moving to Argentina, for instance. Migration is now a global phenomenon affecting nearly all countries of the world.

Coming as I do from Costa Rica, I am not going to pretend that migration does not have its downsides. But what I would like to do today is to outline some of the key benefits of migration. Too often the media and public debate about migration focuses only on the negative aspects of migration. The reality is that migration brings huge benefits, fueling growth, innovation and entrepreneurship in both the countries people come from and those they move to. When governed humanely to promote safety, order and dignity, migration has endless advantages. It provides opportunities, and raise incomes and living standards. These benefits are important to keep in mind because in Europe, where more, not less, migration will probably be needed in the future. Europe's population is aging and the EU is predicting a massive shortage of workers of 45 million in the next 50 years as the working age population will drop. With no further migration to the EU, the population of the EU 27 will be 58 million less than it was in 2010 according to Eurostat data. Contrary to public perceptions that European countries do not need migrants, the reality is that migrants mitigate the effects of an aging and shrinking population and will be key in the sustainability of the dependency rates.

Because of this reason, let me start by the benefits that migration brings to the countries of destination and try to dispel some of the myths that exist.

A particularly strong misconception is that the EU does not need low-skilled immigrants. On the contrary, low-skilled migrants contribute to the functioning of the European economy by taking up jobs undesirable to natives, which in turns allows natives to take up higher-skilled and more remunerative employment. OECD forecasts show that for some countries like Italy, sectors requiring a low-skilled workforce like home care as well as food preparation and services will continue to grow. In other words, low-skilled workers will be needed just as highly skilled ones. Elsewhere, like in the Gulf Cooperation Council countries, migrants make up 90 per cent of the workforce, so these economies would simply collapse without migrants.

That migrants steal native jobs is another unfounded belief. This misconception is more common in countries where unemployment is higher, and countries with high unemployment rates most often appear to be the ones with lower, not higher immigration rates: this could be due, among other reasons, to the fact that migrants move where they are more likely to find jobs and away from countries with higher unemployment.

Moreover, migrants are net positive contributors to the welfare systems of almost every European country, meaning that they contribute to public finances more than they take out in public benefits and services, as confirmed by data from OECD. Migrant households contribute an average 5,000 Euros per year to host countries' public purse, in contrast with frequent accusations of being "benefit tourist" undermining European countries" welfare systems. More broadly, studies show that the fiscal impact of immigration is small and moderate and that it strongly depends on the local context. For instance, studies for the UK indicate that the fiscal impact of migration in the country for the period 2007 -2009 was of 0.46 % of the GDP, greater than in other OECD countries. Immigrants in the UK are less likely to be in social housing than people born in the UK, even when they come from poorer countries. A study by the Bertelsmann Foundation shows that each migrant in Germany contributed 3,300 euros in 2012 on average. In other words, if anything, immigrants make recipient countries slightly richer, never poorer.

Furthermore, migrants enhance rather than restrict the innovation capacity of host societies. Patent applications in Europe are higher in countries with policies to attract highly skilled migrants. The presence of highly-skilled migrants and foreign students in higher education contributes to the creation of knowledge as well, and evidence shows that immigrants increase patterning activity of natives too. Networks of diaspora members contribute to the diffusion of knowledge and the presence of a more diverse workforce makes innovation more likely. Migrants file the majority of patents by leading science firms-65% at Merck, 64 % at General Electric and 60 % at Cisco, just to give a few examples.

Another positive and often overlooked aspect of migration is that migrants are entrepreneurs and create jobs for migrants and natives alike. Companies such as Google, Intel, PayPal, eBay and Yahoo' have all been co-founded by migrants. Migrants have started 25 % of US venture-capital-backed public companies and 40 % of venture-capital-backed technology firms. In 2 out of 4 of all engineering and technology companies established in the US between 1995 and 2005, there was at least one immigrant key founder. These companies were responsible for generating more than 52 billion dollars' worth of sales and creating almost half a million jobs as of 2005. Such contributions have only increased in the past decade. Immigrant firm founders tend to have advanced education in Science, Technology, Engineering and Mathematics and high rates of entrepreneurship and innovation.

Migrants also complement local labour force rather than competing with it by providing skills at all levels and labour force that are needed in most developed countries. An analysis of 30 countries by Hays revealed that many of them, including the US, Mexico, Canada, Chile, Brazil, China, Spain, the UK, France, and Sweden, are facing a " talent mismatch", which means that the available labour force does not have the skills employers are looking for. Research from the Boston Consulting Group suggests that Germany could experience a labour shortage of up to 2.4million by 2020, and Australia of 2.3 mil-

lion. But this is not only true for developed countries. A recent report by the McKinsey Global Institute estimated that by 2020, there will be a 38-40 million potential shortage of workers with higher education globally, and a 45 million shortage of workers with secondary education in developing countries. More high-skill workers will be needed in China, and more medium-skilled workers will be in demand in developing economies of South Asia and sub-Saharan Africa.

Migrants, and especially skilled migrants contribute to increased trade and investment flows between countries of origin and destination, in a way that is beneficial to both; research finds that discrimination might be a constraint to these effects entering into full action, and the fight against discrimination starts, again, with knowledge and understanding of how migrants contribute to societies in destination countries.

When talking about migrants' contribution to society at the global level, we cannot bypass the contributions they make to their countries of origin. It is indeed becoming increasingly difficult to separate contributions to migrants' countries of origin from those in countries of destination, given how interconnected we all are in this globalized world; migrants themselves contribute to making these connections stronger, moving between home and host countries, often temporarily, and building transnational networks.

A critical element: the money sent by migrants back home-404 billion dollars in 2013 according to latest World Bank estimates- dwarfs development aid figures. Remittances are "the most immediate and tangible benefit of international migration", as Kofi Annan once put it. They mean higher health and education expenditures for households who stay behind; better access to information and communication technologies as well as formal financial services; and they provide a cushion in the event of adverse environmental shocks.

Despite the well-known challenges that the "brain drain" present to developing countries, what is often not mentioned is that emigration of highly skilled professionals serves as an incentive for natives to acquire more education that they would have without the prospect of migration. An empirical study on 127 developing countries shows that doubling high-skilled emigration prospects multiplies the proportion of highly skilled natives in those countries by 1.054 after 10 years, and by 1.226 in the long run. Emigration of highly skilled individuals from countries in the Pacific region makes more people willing to acquire tertiary education in those countries. I think that we need to understand better how countries can collaborate to reduce costs and increase benefits of highly skilled emigration, for instance through programs of temporary return of highly skilled migrants resident abroad for skills transfer and training to promote " brain circulation", similar to the ones implemented by IOM.

On the other hand, migrants can also decide to return and increasingly do so. People return with a rich baggage of skills and experiences to contribute in their home countries, meaning emigration can ultimately be good for developing countries. Moreover, migrant's' intentions to return do not only depend on a pure financial calculus and surveys among migrants indicate the frequent intention to return, for example for Indian medical doctors in the UK, or among the best students in Tonga, Papa New Guinea and New Zealand.

Migrants also facilitate the flow of goods, factors and knowledge between origin and destination countries and establish fruitful networks which are beneficial to their communities of origin. One of the most striking cases of the positive contributions of diaspora is given by the rise of the IT sector in India in the 1990s- a real IT revolution-through brain circulation, return migration and the contribution to formal institutions and networks of experts abroad. Indians headed 9 % of Silicon Valley start-ups at the end of the 1990s, mostly in the software sector. There is evidence that skilled migration helps increase foreign investment in migrants' countries. The creation of transnational scientific networks between members of the diaspora contributes to the diffusion of technology across countries. The Chinese diaspora is also a prime example of how knowledge is transferred across countries of origin and destination thanks to the presence of nationals abroad, and how this makes manufacturing activities more productive in the home countries.

In sum, although highly skilled individuals leaving a country represent a loss of human capital, gains for communities in the countries of origin from having highly skilled nationals' abroad need also to be acknowledged.

Lastly, but as importantly, let me briefly talk about migrants' contribution to their own lives. Consider a sample fact. A research from Branko Milanovic suggests that more than 80 % of a person's likely income in the future is determined by two elements only: the individual's country of birth and the income class of her or his parents. If this is true, this means that an individual's personal characteristics and capacity are altogether less relevant to predict how well off the individual will be in the future on a global scale than the county where she or he happens to be born. Migration then becomes eventually the most effective way for people to have better opportunities ahead of them. Workers from developing countries who move to the US earn four times as much as they would have at home to do exactly the same job. Moving from Malawi to South Africa more than doubles the wage of a nurse. Thai workers moving to Taiwan or Hong Kong earn at least four times as much as they would in Thailand.

Of course, higher earnings are just part of the story. People obviously migrate to improve their livelihoods as well as those of their families. The effect of migration on migrant well-being was the focus of IOM's World Migration Report 2013. Based on data from the Gallup World Poll, the report shows that migration improves various aspects of the well-being of migrants across a range of dimensions. Migrants in the North, particularly those who migrated from the North, are those who are better off in terms of life evaluation, finances and health, and they tend to rate their lives better than if they had not migrated. While migrants in the South are better off financially, they rate their well-being similarly or worse than if they had not migrated. Furthermore, migrants in developed countries report less trouble in affording food and shelter than if they had not migrated, although the picture is not so positive for migrants moving across developing countries. Importantly, migration improves migrants' health outcomes when comparing migrants to those who stayed behind.

I hope to have convinced all of you that migrants greatly contribute to home and host societies in a variety of ways. However, we should not forget that such contributions sometimes come at a very high cost for migrants. Dispelling the many and all too common myths and misconceptions about migration is essential if we are to maximize the benefits of migration for all involved actors. That is why IOM has launched the Migrants Contribute campaign. The countering of misinformation to make the case for migration requires a strong evidence base, and making sure that the facts are presented in a way that people understand. Better evidence, data and evaluations of the impact of migration policies and programmes are essential if we are to counter misconceptions about the real scale and impact of migration.

It is only then, that politicians will be able to develop fact-based policies and legislative frameworks that respond to the real needs while promoting the protection and integration of migrants in host societies.

Also Florence Jaumote, Ksenia Koloskova and Sweta Saxena said no matter how controversial politically, migration makes sense economically. In addition, a new IMF study shows that over the longer term, both high-and-low-skilled workers who migrate bring benefits to their new home countries by increasing income per person and living standards. High-skilled migrants bring diverse talent and expertise, while low-skilled migrants fill essential occupations for which natives are in short supply and allow natives to be employed at higher-skilled jobs. Moreover, the gains are broadly shared by the population. It may therefore be well-worth shouldering the short-term costs to help integrate these new workers.

The report indicated that migration is nothing new. According to the report, rhetoric surrounding migration has turn more negative in recent years. Yet, migration is not a new phenomenon. While the recent refugee surge has made it a hot-button issue, advanced economies already have a large and growing population of migrants. They contribute 15 to 20 percent of the working-age population in many advanced economies, and around 30 percent in some Anglo-Saxon countries such as Australia and New Zealand. Between 1990 and 2015, immigrants accounted for half of the growth in working age population of advanced economies. They are essential to ensure the future workforce in most advanced economies, where the working-age population would shrink over the next decade without further immigration.

It stated that while the stock of low-skilled migrants has been the largest (and broadly constant in percent of adult population over time), the share of high-skilled has been on the rise. Anglo-Saxon countries tend to have a higher population of high-skilled migrants than continental European and Nordic countries.

As migrants on average tend to be younger than their adopted county's native-born population, they help increase the share of working age population. This is the best known channel through which migration increases income per person. But as this new study shows, it is by far not the most important one.

The study found that the most important channel through which the arrival of migrant workers affects income per person is by increasing labour productivity.

- *Migrants increases Gross Domestic Product (GDP) per person and Productivity: A 1 percentage point increase in the share of migrants in the adult population increases GDP per person in advanced economies by up to 2 percent in the longer term according to the study. This increase comes primarily from an increase in labour productivity, instead of an increase in the workforce-to-population ratio.*

- *Both high-and low-skilled migrants improve productivity: The gains migrants bring are not exclusive to high-skilled workers with specific knowledge and diverse skills according to the study. Low-skilled migrants also have a significant impact on overall productivity by complementing the existing skills set of the population.*

- *Low-skilled migrants fill essential occupations for which the native-born population is in short supply, contributing to a more efficient functioning of the economy;*

- *When low-skilled migrants take up more manual routine tasks, the native-born population tend to move to more complex occupation that require language and communication skills in which they have a comparative advantage; and*

- *In what is a key example of complementarity, low-skilled migrants provide housekeeping and childcare services (the "nanny effect") and thus allow native-born women to return to work, or work longer hours.*

According to the study, immigration can bring substantial benefits to advanced economies in terms of higher per capita GDP and standards of living. These gains are broadly shared by the population. But the key to reaping these benefits is to address the challenges posed by migration in the short term and, in particular, to ensure migrants are integrated into the labour market.

The policies to accomplish this include: language training, job search support, better recognition of the education and work experience of migrants, and lower barriers to entrepreneurship. While integrating migrants can add to fiscal cost pressures in the short run, these policies allow migrants to obtain and keep a job at a relevant skill level, and increasingly contribute to the fiscal accounts.

At the time, native workers, too, require some help to adjust, including by upgrading their skills. Policymakers also need to avoid possible overburdening of public services such as health care and education to contain possible buildup of social tensions.

While migrants bring benefit to the host countries as well as sending countries, the developed countries should welcome people and allow them to enjoy the freedom to search a better life.

Police scuffling with migrants

As more economic and political instability arises in Africa and other parts of the world, the movement of poor and vulnerable people in search of protection and economic well-being migration will continue. People are forced to leave because they lack confidence to stay in their countries where there are too many troubles. It is the same reason many young men and women from The Gambia flee the country during the Second Republic. It is true to say that almost every family in The Gambia has one of its son, daughter, cousin, brother, sister or niece that left on a bus for Niger before their destination in Libya where they tried to cross to Europe across the Mediterranean Sea.

These young men and women took the risk to leave The Gambia in search of greener pastures. Besides paying bus fares from Banjul to Niger, they pay extortionate bribes in Niger according to some returnees, only to wait for a smuggler bound for Libya where they endure real inhumane treatment in the hands of bandits or street gangs. While in Libya, they are taken to farms where they are used like slaves. Because they were sold, their masters used them on the farm like animals with little regard for their health. They said some of them were gun-butted by their masters for just working slow on the farms. They said because they had to comply fully they worked as dictated while relying on prayers for God to help them escape.

According to them, it took several attempts before they could escape but again they were captured and taken to a more heinous detention centre where they were always beaten for almost three months. They only left that detention centre thanks to International Organization for Migration that rescued them. Before leaving Libya they met some of their colleagues who were in Tripoli and told them about similar bitter experiences in the hands of bandits. Those from other detention centres told them how the Libyan police raided illegal-migrants and took them to detention centres where they were seriously beaten. They said like many of their colleagues that finally returned to The Gambia, they saw in Libya the worse inhumane treatment that any human can imagine to happen in the 21st century.

According to them, instead of some countries in the European Union talking about strengthening their borders to prevent migrants from entering their countries, they should visit Libya and see the cruel treatment done to the innocent and vulnerable people in the hands of both Libyan police and gangs. They said only someone who experienced the cruel treatment would tell you exactly what migrants faced in the hands of gangs while in Libya. The migrants, according to them, are people that only left their countries because of civil war, poverty, persecution and human right abuses. They were looking for protection and a better life that could help them earn a living and help their families back home. They said it was sad that despite the fact that the people risked their lives across the desert they ended up in detention centres where they were treated like animals.

They urged the world powers to act now to avoid loss of generations in Libya and the Mediterranean Sea where lots of people die while attempting to cross to Europe. They said migrants all over; especially those who travelled across the Mediterranean Sea by boats should be given all the necessary support in terms of employment opportunities and better shelter. These migrants according to them make their ways through the dangerous 'back-way' journey by crossing the Mediterranean Sea by wooden and rubber boats some of which capsized, killing Africans teeming youth in large numbers. They said that most of the boats that capsized are never reported on the media. They believe lots of lives are loss in the deadly Mediterranean Sea route to Europe than accounted for. According to them, even those that were migrating by road, they were stuck in the desert and killed by hunger and thirst. They told me that there were instances some people drank their urine as water only to dehydrate to death. According to them, it is important for the world powers to know facts about the 'back way' in order to help the desperate people who are taking the route because they have no hope of better lives in their home countries.

Like many other returnees from Libya, the story given by these groups of people made me cry because of the sympathy I have for innocent young men and women that were going through pain after they left home due to economic hardship and insecurity in their home countries. As I cry, I call on the world powers to rescue poor people from poverty and insecurity. Also, let the world powers grant freedom and protection to migrants in their countries. Poor people only need employment opportunities and security to live a dignified life. Let the developed countries always know that it is the migrants who take up jobs that native-born are in short supply and at the same time contribute to the economies of their countries by paying taxes.

5

Youth Need Entrepreneurial Development to Stop 'Back-Way' Migration

The high rate of unemployment and constant political instability across Africa continue to frustrate the youth. They waited so long to see positive changes in the way governments govern the people but are disappointed that after so many years of waiting African governments cannot address unemployment matters and stop unnecessary civil wars. Because they no longer have confidence in the way their leaders operate coupled with lots of flimsy excuses when it comes to creating employment opportunities for the youth, they shifted their original status of being very patient to taking risk of travelling through the 'back way' to Europe in search of a better life and security. It is a fact Africa has a youthful population many of whom has acquired acceptable education but remains unemployed due to lack of job opportunities. It is sad that many African governments cannot provide employment opportunities for the youth. It was the lack of employment and resources to start entrepreneurial programmes that forced the youth to look for alternative to survive such as to embark on perilous 'back-way' journey in search of job opportunities elsewhere in the developed countries.

Evidently, the youth of Africa play crucial role in putting leaders in position by voting as they form the huge part of the population. Because their votes usually form the large part of the total votes required for someone to win a political seat politicians greatly rely on them in their run-up to the elections. Every politician, particularly, the presidential candidates count on youth greatly in order to win the election. These politicians normally give all sorts of promises to the youth, especially to provide employment opportunities during the political campaign so as to win their minds to vote for them. However, most promises made to the youth during political campaign are usually not honoured by the same politicians after they win the election. This is always sad as it discourages the youth. Like most parts of the world, African youth support politicians on the basis that they will improve the living condition of their people by providing them with employment opportunities, good health care, drinking water, electricity and market for their agricultural products but in many cases the youth get disappointed.

It is a fact that many youth of African have attractive talents in various disciplines such as carpentry, Welding, masonry, tailoring, plumbing etc, but because they lack financial support to help them establish well in terms of getting the necessary tools they end up using their physical powers working hard and not earning any decent income. Just like the professions mentioned, there are many African youth with talents in other professions such as musicians, entertainers, dancers, hoteliers, waiters and cooking. The majority of the people in this category also spend their valuable time working hard and performing without earning a decent income. It is sad that most of the people in the second category usually do not even receive proper attention from society because they are not seen to have the income necessary to inspire other people. Actually, it is only the people that have travelled far and wide and see the importance of professions like cooking and entrainment who respect such professions. These professions should be given the necessary attention by providing the necessary support in terms of the atmosphere that could help the performers to showcase their talents and earn a decent income.

African youth are really trying to earn a living in the most difficult conditions. To know this, you just need to take a walk or drive along the roads in many parts of Africa and see for yourself the various professions youth are engaged in for survival. They work hard day and night but they do not earn good income. Alongside the difficulties of getting the necessary tools to work with, they usually lack good customers to buy the little materials they make to sell so as to get income. It is sad that many carpentry, tailoring and mechanic workshops have more than ten people all of whom depend on their bosses for lunch and pocket money to take home when the total earnings in those workshops are usually less than one thousand five dalasis daily (just 34 US Dollars).

Considering the low income received from their work coupled with family pressures makes many youth to look for alternatives to support themselves and their families. It was out of this frustration that leads to the mass exodus through the 'back way' to Europe. To be sure about this, I visited several workshops around the Greater Banjul Area during the Second Republic and the tour made me know exactly that many youth left through the 'back way' in search of a better life because they were earning relatively low income despite the hard work while their families depended on them for feeding, paying school fees and medical care for the sick and elderly. It is unfortunate that many youth still use their physical power in the 21st century to make materials such as wooden bed, chairs, tables, ward-drop and even doors and with all the efforts they end up earning almost nothing.

Africa needs the basic technology that is being used by the developed countries to make furniture and other materials for human use. The continent needs to help save the physical power of its people. Truly, Africans are intelligent as they use their physical power to turn things around positively. It is absolutely amazing to see the creative work done by Africans in the absence of technology. Look at mechanics, for example, and see how they manually dismantle the entire parts of cars and fix mechanical problems before reassembling the parts making cars roadworthy again. It is in the same way that Africans dismantle any forms of hand cells (mobile phones) fix problems as well as unlocked phones made with the use of technology to enable users to enjoy the services. These extraordinary skills acquired by many Africans mean the people are intelligent and only needs the necessary technology and trainings to enable them to move the world for better.

It is absolutely sad though to see a highly skilled African working almost twenty-hours without earning a decent income. Because the highly-skilled Africans continue to get frustrated the majority decide to leave through the 'back way' in search of a better life elsewhere. The mass exodus of both highly- skilled and low-skilled Africans to Europe and other parts of the world causes serious brain drain on the continent. They continue to move despite the fact that they are usually not welcomed in Europe and elsewhere even though they contribute significantly to the Gross Domestic Product of their destinations by paying the taxes from their meagre resources. These people usually take up casual jobs that the natives are always in short supply and work tirelessly with little pay. They do that because they have no choice.

I ask whether it makes sense to disapprove people's presence in a country where they contribute to the development of the economy. I ask because it is exactly the case when it comes to migrants in most developed countries. Most countries in the European Union and America continue to refuse to recognize migrants despite the dirty jobs they do and contributions they make to their economies. It is always shocking to read in the media that a particular developed country plans to deport migrants. Anytime I listen to announcements about a strong economy trying to deport migrants I usually ask myself whether the world has any more historians that could tell people that migration is a long phenomenon that cannot be erased. Can someone make the strong economies know that they got developed because of the contributions of the people, including migrants that took up dirty jobs and paid taxes that added up to their Gross Domestic product (GDP)?

The majority of Africans who travel to Europe and America for studies and related matters would tell you the kind of jobs many Africans do to earn a living. The majority of migrants work as security guards, tellers at supermarkets, cooks and dish washers at restaurants, clean roads, grounds, supermarkets, restaurants and even train and bus stops. They also take up jobs such as babysitter, daycare for the elderly as well as building constructions. Trust me, no matter what time you wake up at night you will see a black or other migrants working in the streets of London either to empty dumping bins or cleaning at the train station. It is sad that they work in terribly cold situations, especially during the snowfall. Despite doing the terrible work that is usually low paid, they pay high taxes to their host countries. Unfortunately, these people have no choice than to work on terrible conditions with less respect for their human dignity because they could not get a better employment and protection in their home countries.

Migrants working at train station

It is painful to know that despite Africans and other migrants from developing countries doing casual jobs and working under terrible situations, they in many cases encounter discrimination because of their colour. Trust me, not every black or other migrant receives a better human treatment in Europe and other developed countries around the world. While a few enjoy, the majority are involved in dally fracas with either employers or supervisors most of whom look low on them despite their contribution in sustaining their business through paying taxes to the host country. It is a fact to say that almost all the casual jobs in Europe, America and other developed countries are sustained and survived by migrants who not only work to promote such jobs by paying taxes that enables the host countries recognize such firms they also promote the image of those jobs by defending firms even when it lacks standard. Honestly, it is very rare to see a native-English or American taking up casual job. Interestingly, despite the fact that migrants help improve the economies of the developed countries some natives continue to refuse to recognize migrants, especially the black as their fellow human beings who left their countries in search of protection.

As most developed countries continue to refuse to accept migrants I urge African leaders to shift their attention from negotiating mere travel opportunities for the politicians alone to work on promoting entrepreneurship development programmes for the youth of Africa. While I strongly believe that the issue of people migrating is not going to go away knowing the history of human migration, I think African leaders should engage their partners in the developed countries to support entrepreneurship development for African youth to enable them to get better training so as to take up initiates that would held them earn a better living.

This is important because it will help Africa retain its human capital, thus preventing further brain drain. Also, the incomes that would be generated by the youth after acquiring entrepreneurial skills would add up to the economy thereby creating more job opportunities. Trust me; migrants would continue to be subjected to unequal treatment so long as there is lack of understanding or acknowledgement about the benefits migrants bring to their host countries, their sending countries as well as to themselves. In most cases, the issue of migrants is viewed in the context of people sending remittances to back home alone. While that is part of it, people should understand the fact that migrants contribute immensely to economies of their host countries by paying taxes.

As the debate on whether to send migrants back to their native countries continues, I urge for support to promote entrepreneurship development for the youth of Africa. For the purpose of helping the reader understand what I am talking about I deem it important to define entrepreneurship, which simply means the ability and preparedness to develop, organize and manage a business venture along with any of its risks in order to make a profit. The most obvious examples of entrepreneurship are the starting of new business. Entrepreneurial life-force is characterized by invention and risk-taking, and is a critical part of a nation's capability to succeed in an ever changing and increasingly economical global marketplace.

The perception of an entrepreneur is developed when principles and terms from a business, managerial, and personal understanding are considered. Almost all the definitions of entrepreneurship, there is agreement that we are taking about a kind of behaviour that includes:

- Enterprise talking
- The establishing and regrouping of social and economic mechanisms to turn resources and situations to practical account and
- Recognition of risk or failure

Because many youth in most developing countries lack the proper education on business development and the use of information and communication technology, they cannot compete in the job market. Lack of this opportunity is one of the major reasons the youth embark on the mass exodus through the 'back way' to Europe in search of greener pastures. To ensure that African youth stay on the continent by completely doing away with the perilous 'back-way' journey to Europe, the developed countries need to assist the governments of the developing countries with entrepreneurship development programmes to enhance the capacities of the youth with business opportunities, self-employment, and employability. Furthermore, the developed countries also need to help the developing countries with the know-how in improving and monitoring the administrative environment to promote competitive entrepreneurial activities in the formal sector, including through broad-based curriculum development programmes for entrepreneurship education and skills training.

I urge the developed countries to support the youth of Africa with entrepreneurial programmes that could help them acquire the relevant knowledge and skills they need to succeed in the world of work. The move will undoubtedly help youth unlock their potential through access to decent work that will drive progress towards sustainable, comprehensive development. It is sad that there are thousands of youth in most African countries that are unemployed -or underemployed. The situation is even worse in the case of young girls who continue to face greater challenges in securing productive and prosperous employment. The European Union instead of making policy to strengthen the presence of naval forces in the Mediterranean Sea to curb the movement of people trying to reach Europe should do the following:

- Develop a comprehensive policy on youth economic empowerment to support developing countries. The move will undoubtedly provide the means for European Union action to be targeted at ensuring that youth have the opportunities to learn the skills and get the experiences they need to succeed in the world of employment.

- Focus on supporting the developing countries with funds to open entrepreneurial programmes that could promote youth engagements in knowledge and skills acquisition so as to increase their access to the labour market, to microfinance and to the economic assets and resources necessary to be active in the labour market.

- Work with developing countries, through funding and interchange, to create opportunities and provide youth with the skills needed to secure better employment.

- Assist the developing countries with experts in youth development and working tools that would help youth utilize their full potentials and get better jobs that will bring attractive incomes for them.

- Promote investment in the economies of the developing countries so that governments can have the necessary resources to create manufacturing companies that could hire lots of youth.

- Help developing countries with projects that could help improve education system, such as research, teacher training and curriculum design. The move will help youth acquire better education thereby stand a better chance to get good employment.

Promoting employment opportunities for the youth should be given priority in order to curb the mass exodus through the dangerous 'back-way' journeys to Europe. Africa cannot do it alone due to the limited financial and material resources necessary to create employment opportunities. It is the reason the developed countries should partner with the developing countries in this campaign to prove that the world powers are serious about addressing the migration issues. Let the everyone understand that so long as inequality in access to national cake exists coupled with rapid unemployment, insecurity, poverty and persecution people affected will always seek for better protection elsewhere they think is stable.

It is an open secret that unemployment in most developing countries is soaring while at the same time their economies are getting worse. So long as the developing countries continue to battle with economic hardship its people will continue to leave in search of greener pasture. To solve the mass movement of poor and vulnerable people across political boundaries requires the developed countries to partner with the developing countries in the areas of promoting entrepreneurial skills for the youth. The move will help the developing countries create opportunities of its youth thereby enabling them engage in meaningful programmes necessary to improve their living conditions.

As the developing countries battle with unemployment issues for the youth coupled with the desire for youth empowerment, education and employments, the former United Nations Secretary General Ban Ki-Moon once told World Leaders and dignitaries at high-level event on the demographic dividend and youth empowerment held at United Nations Headquarters in New York that "the world has the largest generation of young people in history.

He said he placed great hope in the youth power to shape our future". Mr. Ban said much the world is poised experience a demographic dividend –the economic growth that can occur when a population shifts from one with many dependents and comparatively few working-ages people to one many working –age people with fewer dependents.

To realize the dividend according to him requires countries to invest in the empowerment, education and employment of their young people. He said there were 1.8 billion young people in the world during his tenure in office, which represented overwhelming amount of human potential. Yet too many of them are stuck in poverty, with few opportunities to learn or to earn a decent living. "We all appreciate the massive waste of human capital in our world when 74 million young people cannot find work", said former Secretary General Mr. Ban.

Young people are hungry for better options. "They are refusing the status quo and demanding a better future. Many of them are demanding their rights to a decent living, and they are willing to take risks to do so. We have seen in recent times the high number of young people taking risks around the Mediterranean, trying to reach a better life," said Dr Babatunde Osotimehin, executive Director of the United Nations Population Fund, UNFPA. But if these youth are allowed to realize their full potential, developing countries according to him could see huge economic gains.

"The more young people grow into well-educated adults with fewer dependents and new opportunities to acquire wealth, savings and purchasing power, the more they will be able to accelerate economic growth and development," said Sam K Kutesa, President of the 69th Session of the General Assembly, who convened the high-level event with support from UNFPA and the International Labour Organization. "It is estimated the African continent could add up to about $500 billion per year to its economy for as many as 30 years," Mr Kutesa further indicated.

As the convergence proposed way forward for youth development the following points were stated by different experts:

- Dr Osotimehin said there are clear steps that can help countries achieve a demographic dividend. Countries need to increase investment in young people. Provide a diversity of training for them-from quality primary and secondary schools to technical training to two-year College and to research-intensive universities. Also essential is "empowering women and girls, and ensuring their sexual and reproductive health and human rights," he indicated.

- Daniel Johnson, Minister of Youth, Sports and Culture of the Bahamas, said countries must also increase employment opportunities for young people. "Many young people will be forced to sit on margins of society, waiting on the train track for a train that may never come," he said, referring to the lack of employment options available in many communities.

- There is also a critical need to involve young people in decision that will affect them. "We cannot talk about sustainable development without the active involvement of youth." Mr Ban Ki-Moon said adding: "when we give young people decent jobs, political weight, negotiating muscle, and real influence in our world, they will create a better future."

Because the developing countries lack the necessary resources to fully support youth empowerment through knowledge and skills acquisition to access to employment and market, the developed countries should help by providing entrepreneurship programmes for the youth of Africa through governments. The programmes should be aimed at generally and economically empower disadvantage youth and women in market oriented technical, entrepreneurial and managerial skills, confidence building and empowering new skills to improve their accessibility to fruitful resources and maintainable earning potential. Also, necessary training to youth is vital as it will improve their knowhow in technology, microfinance and a better access to market.

There have to be programmes that could take market-led approach to improve the skills and create employment opportunities of the youth to enable them to utilize fully their potential. The move will give confidence to youth particularly the returning migrants the majority of whom are left without money and valuable assets at home as they had already sold their assets with the hope of reaching their dreamland where they expected a lot in terms of opportunities to improve their living condition. I believe an immediate action should be taken to support the returnees and other youth by providing entrepreneurial development programmes for them. The move will help them to engage in productive venture that could assist in alleviating their condition, particularly their economic status. More returns without work opportunities simply means there will be frustration.

While the whole world believes that education, including learning how to access and stay in work, is vital to empowering the youth to make the crucial evolution from school to work, and from childhood to independent adult citizens of their environments, people need to understand that without economic well-being it will be difficult to realize the dream of making the youth happy. It is sad that even in the 21st century, many African youth on the continent continue to fight to gain better education and to get a good job. This is the case because in many developing countries, the education systems usually fail to equip the youth with the right skills they need for adult life. This is because many education systems lack the necessary skilled lecturers and teaching materials that could help improve the learning condition of the people.

It is also sad that despite all good intentions of some African leaders to enhance the living conditions of the youth, many developing countries lack the necessary financial resources to fix the problems affecting the youth. The word powers need to know that the developing countries are committed to the promotion of the living conditions of their youth to enable them stay in their continent and contribute to the development of their countries. It was the reason the President of the republic of the Gambia Mr. Adama Barrow in his maiden speech at the United Nations General Assembly in New York on 19 September 2017 mentioned the difficult challenges many poor youth of African were faced with that contributed to the mass movement of people through the dangerous back way journey.

The full text of Mr. Barrow speech reads:

Mr. President

Mr. Secretary General

Yours Majesties

Your Excellences –Heads of State and Government

Distinguished Ladies and Gentlemen

With warm greetings to you all from the New Gambia, we thank the Almighty God for making this great gathering of global leaders possible once again this year. Allow me to formally congratulate the President of the General Assembly and the Secretary General of our congratulation for their leadership and commitment to the values of the United Nations.

After more than seventy years of existence, the United Nations undoubtedly remains the ultimate international platform for finding solutions to global challenges, as we in The Gambia know all too well. Today, being my maiden appearance at this great forum of world leaders, let me take this opportunity to re-affirm The Gambia's firm commitment to the Charter of the United nations. My Government fully appreciates the UN's central role in the pursuit of preventive diplomacy to avert crises around the world.

Mr President

The recent political crisis that took place in my country created a new democratic beginning and the experience taught us useful lessons that Gambians will not easily forget. We learnt that will power and national unity, decisive regional intervention as well as undivided and clear support of the international community could produce positive outcomes. Also of importance, was the coordinated international action inspired by our common values of solidarity, democracy, respect for human rights and the rule of law which was critical in sending the right message to the former President to respect the will of the people and leave without bloodshed.

During those difficult times, we know we had friends, ones who came to our aid and who have since kept faith with us. We therefore would like to seize this great opportunity to thank the leaders of ECOWAS for their firm intervention in bringing peace to The Gambia. We also thank our regional and international friends who stood by us in our critical hour of need. Thanks to your collective efforts, The Gambia is now on a solid path to peace and good governance and ready to take over our traditional role among the champions of human rights and democracy. Gambians have made an irreversible choice to close a dark chapter in our history and today our national agenda is one of reform and transformation.

Like any restored democracy, we are facing enormous challenges in the revival of our economy, a comprehensive reform of our laws, our administrative and judicial institutions. The modernization of our security sector, consolidation of the rule of law and human rights are part of our reform programme. It is only by overcoming these challenges that we can reinforce our democratic gains and my government is committed to delivering a New Gambia that is fit for our children to be proud of. Indeed young people were all along at the forefront of our democratic transition and addressing youth unemployment, which is a top priority of my government, will no doubt create enormous opportunities.

Mr President

We also recognize the crucial role of Gambians in the diaspora in contributing to the transformation of our motherland. let me seize this opportunity to sincerely thank our development partners and friends for the invaluable budget and policy support they are providing to the Government to help address the challenges of job creation and youth irregular migration. My government is committed to using such resources wisely for sustainable socio-economic development.

Mr President

We may be small country but one with huge needs. As a matter of urgent priority, we have develop a New National Development Plan in line with the transformative agenda of the new Government. This development blueprint is designed to put the country back to economic growth and prosperity following two decades of mismanagement, corruptions, and widespread human rights violations. The new plan is built on sound macro-economic and fiscal policies that will lead to stability and economic growth over the medium and long term. It has also incorporated the Sustainable Development Goals and other commitments contained in Agenda 2030 and the Paris Agreement on Climate Change.

The Paris Agreement is critically relevant for The Gambia because climate change means a lot more in our situation. When land productivity declines and water shortage intensifies, young people from rural areas are often sent away to ease the burden on the family and to find new sources of income. This sadly explains why many young Gambians have been forced to make the long and dangerous journey to Europe. The journey is so risky that many perish at high seas and never reach their final destination. Countless others disappear into immigration detention centres or vanish in the sands of the Sahara desert.

Those who are able to complete the journey are often dismissed as economic migrants and sent back home. This sense of hopelessness and frustration also provides fertile ground for smugglers and extremist groups to recruit innocent youths into the criminal underworld. Young people do not deserve this experience; they deserve the chance to enjoy a state and prosperous future at home. Creating new employment opportunities that provide young people with sustainable incomes and connect them to a revitalized land, healthy and productive environment is an investment in the future of the nation. This is a key priority in our National Development Plan.

Over the last decade, we lost many of our friends and development partners through wrong policy choices, but since the restoration of democracy and good governance, many of our long-standing partners are coming back to work with us. We are also committed to be part of the African Peer Review Mechanism. We are finalizing plans for a roundtable donor conference to mobilize resources for the long –term development of the country. Your continued support, solidarity and partnership will be critical to the success of that conference.

Mr President

Although The Gambia did not go through armed conflict, the political crisis that we experienced came as a result of decades of bad governance, weak state institutions, rule of fear, and growing intolerance. We were on the brink of political violence and armed conflict. We therefore express our deep apprecia-

tion to the United Nations Office for West Africa, United Nations Peace Building Commission and the Peace Building Support Office for the initial critical support that they have rendered to my country. Your continued support in the areas of transitional justice and security sector reform will certainly go a long way towards entrenching peace, justice and democracy in The Gambia.
Mr President

There is neither a shortage of ideas nor that of resources to fix the major problems facing the human race. What has always been scare is the political will and unless adequate resources are invested, the pace of development will remain slow and minimal impact achieved. It is against that backdrop that I am calling on the private sector to emulate philanthropies for their generosity towards the most isolated, marginalized and deprived sections of the world, providing safe drinking water, roads, power, healthcare and education, key to regarding human dignity.
Mr President

The pursuit of peace and security in Africa and the world will always be a major foreign policy goal for The Gambia. We will pursue good neighborliness and cooperation with the sister Republic of Senegal and the countries of ECOWAS will remain strategic partners. West Africa is on the march towards the consolidation of its democratic gains but as a region we are facing serious threats to our peace and security. Terrorism, extremism, religious intolerance, organized crime and drug trafficking are seriously undermining our development efforts. Recent attacks in Mali, Burkina Faso, Cote d'Ivoire and the Sahel in general underscore the urgent need for greater regional and international cooperation in addressing these challenges.
Mr President

The indifference, the injustice, and the indignities in isolated parts of the world create real threats to global peace, prosperity and democracy. We need to take bigger and bolder steps to close the gap between the North and South as the world is too imbalanced.
Mr President

We remain deeply concerned that the Israeli-Palestinian conflict still defies resolution. My government firmly subscribes to the idea of a two-state solution for the two people to live side by side in peace and harmony. We therefore call on the UN Secretary-General to vigorously pursue this formula in the interest of lasting peace.
Mr President

In our foreign policy and as part of our historic friendship, we fully recognize the one-China policy. The People's Republic of China is the sole representative of the Chinese people and a true friend of The Gambia. Our two countries continue to strengthen cooperation on the basis of a win-win approach built on mutual trust and respect within the framework of the Forum for China-Africa Cooperation.

Mr President

An organization like the United Nations, by virtue of its functions, would always require some level of reform of its management systems. The intergovernmental character of the mandates entrusted to the Secretariat requires the existence of trust and accountability between member states and the Secretariat. As you embark on your proposed reforms, we stand ready to give you our full support in the interest of an effective and more relevant world body.

Lastly, but not the least, one of the long-standing issues is the pending question of Security Council reform. Former Secretary-General Kofi Annan once said that " no reform of the United Nations is complete without reform of the Security Council" That remains true today. Africa will not give up its legitimate and historic quest for true representative on the Council and The Gambia fully supports the African Union's demand for the long overdue reform of the Security Council.

Mr President

I want to conclude by reaffirming my optimism and confidence in our collective ability to uplift mankind from the clutches of poverty, to institute a global order of peace, firmly held together by justice, loving, caring and tolerating each other. In tune with our National Anthem, we pledge our firm allegiance to these values we hold ever true.

With best wishes from the people of The Gambia-the Smiling Coast of Africa, I wish you all a successful 72nd Session of the United Nations General Assembly. God bless the world, thank you.

As great leaders of Africa stood at the UN General Assembly and talked about their desire to help the youth of the Continent through employment creation, the Word powers need to know that the developing countries are committed to the promotion of the living conditions of their youth to enable them stay in their continent and contribute to the development of their countries. However, many countries could not do that because of numerous challenges face with the limited financial resource that is always too small to fix issues such as creation of employment opportunities and better education. Like many developing countries, the government of the republic of the Gambia under the leadership of President Adama Barrow has a vision for youth development. It is the reason the desire for youth empowerment, including providing them a better education is mentioned in almost all his nation address, including the 2017 State Opening of the National Assembly on 24 July 2017, the Coalition's one year anniversary and 2018 New Year's messages.

The full text of the president's state opening of the National Assembly reads:
Service chiefs
Members of the diplomatic and consular corps,
Members of the Media
Fellow Gambians,
Ladies and Gentlemen,
My fellow Gambians,

You have elected the government that you want and we have taken your ex-pressions of goodwill and your desire for peace and prosperity seriously. We have thus begun the task of steadily reforming the government machinery so it can do the work of nation building and help strengthen our new democracy that we have wanted for so long.

I want to offer my thanks to the Economic Community of West African States (ECOWAS), the African Union, the United Nations, the European Union, the World Bank, and all our international partners for their invaluable support in this historic transition. They too have worked with us in the spirit of unity and cooperation to serve the New Gambia.

They have all moved swiftly to help stabilize this nation through support with security and human and financial resources. I know we can count on their continued support particularly to overcome the dire financial situation that we inherited. But ultimately, we Gambians must forge our way along the path of democracy and prosperity. I am proud to say that we are already well on our way in these first few months of our administration

We have got a lot to do in 2017 and beyond and as I have always said, this is going to be a government of action. Our immediate priority is to fix the contin-uous energy problem as well as the broken economy, unify the nation, improve health and agricultural sub -sectors, end the country's isolation and introduce robust institutional, electoral and constitutional reforms in line with our new democratic principles that will respond to the realities of our time. This has to be done in accordance with reforms in the Civil Service and security sector as well as State Owned Enterprises.

A Peaceful Transition

Our most important achievement so far is the peace transition of power to this new democracy. As mentioned earlier, we are indebted to ECOWAS, the AU, the UN, the EU, the World Bank, the IMF and other international part-ners for their support. They have all moved quickly to help stabilize our coun-try with the help of security, human and financial resources.

As the saying goes charity begins at home, so we must acknowledge that we Gambians are to be commended for initiating the change that brought us the New Gambia. We shall continue to build our country together.

Justice and Judiciary

While we have restored some of the key democratic institutions, the pursuit of justice remains a high priority for my government. Indeed, we still have a lot to do despite the progress made so far. Over 500 prisoners have been pardoned and we have delivered on our promise to decongest prison by releasing political and other deserving reformed prisoners

A Criminal Case and Detention Review Panel has also been established to enquire into all criminal proceedings against current and former public officers and panel has uncovered cases linked to political activity, and persons remanded and awaiting trial. We have recently and carefully concluded the work on the setting up of a Commission of Inquiry to look into the financial and business-related activities of the former President and his associates. The members of the Commission chaired by Surahata Semega Janneh have been announced and the Commission will start work shortly.

Additionally, our judiciary has been "Gambianised" with the appointment of a Gambian Chief Justice and Six Superior Court Judges. We also had a successful National Stakeholders' Conference on Justice and Human Rights in May and the forum provided a unique opportunity for inclusive dialogue and consultations on key justice sector reforms, including plans for the setting up of a Truth and Reconciliation Commission.

My government has received and continues to benefit from genuine and solid support provided by the UN in the area of transitional justice and the setting up of this Commission.

Security and Defence

In the area of security and defense, we are grateful for the support of the ECOWAS Mission in the Gambia. The ECOMIG forces were especially instrumental in helping to secure our democratic transition. The government is working on reforming the security sector which is closely linked to the delivery of justice and the restoration of our free and fair democracy.

Gone are the days of armed security personnel representing the face of government. The Gambian Armed Forces are now confined to their military barracks. Members of the former State Guard Battalion have been redeployed to other units, and the armed forces are now disengaged from civilian matters. It is also important to note that arms and ammunitions have been stored in safe locations.

We must, however, applaud our gallant Armed Forces, who have been receptive to the normalization of their role in the state, and have conducted themselves with maximum professionalism. They continue to play a critical role in keeping our nation safe and secure, and deserve our unconditional support and respect as they carry out their professional duties. To ensure that our military remain effective and professional, we plan to set up n infantry centre and school, as well as military academy to train our officers and other personnel in all aspects of military science.

The Former National Intelligence Agency, now the State Intelligence Service, has been restructured to focus on its core activity of intelligence gathering and analysis to ensure the safety and security of us all.

Information and Communications

In the area of information and communications, we have taken concrete steps to review oppressive media laws, to ensure freedom of the press and freedom of expression. These are founding pillars of any strong democracy, and my government has moved quickly to reinstate three private radio shows that were illegally shut down. All these efforts will enhance the quality, the scope and the openness of information, news and the media throughout our country. It is reassuring to now hear and see debates on divergent views expressed freely on radio, on television and in our newspapers.

In one of my recent cabinet meetings we agreed, as an immediate priority, on the need to put in place a communication strategy that will facilitate regular communication and engagements with the public. New communications measures have been introduced to include regular press briefings by the media team at the Office of the President, by the Minister of Information and Communication Infrastructure, and bi-annual news conference by me.

Energy

Turning to the energy sector, let me start by restating the urgency that I attach to resolving the power supply issues across the nation. Electricity is power-the power to support education and learning, the power to run lifesaving health facilities, and the power for businesses to create jobs, and grow the economy.

I came into office to find significant challenges in the energy sector, as is evident in frequent power outages. Electrical power is one of the most basic services that people need for a decent quality of life, and the lack of it greatly affects the net national productivity and lives of the people.

To meet these challenges and tackle our acute power shortage, my government has made it a priority from day one, to work with international partners, investors and developers to attract investments in the energy sector. Some of the negotiations are at a very advanced stage. We recently signed an agreement for a new 60-megawatt power plant, which will more than double the current generation capacity in the country. It will deliver adequate and stable electric power supply in the whole of the Greater Banjul Area. I am also happy to report that the proposal to acquire electricity from our sister Republic of Senegal is well advanced. It is worth to know that this cross-border connection is a short-term measure to boost the energy supply, especially in the rural areas.

Madam Speaker

Regarding the petroleum sub-sector, over the past twenty-two years, Gambians have either been left in the dark or seriously misinformed about petroleum prospects. My government will be transparent and honest about the state of petroleum, and should there be positive results, we are committed to governing the sector with total transparency and accountability.

Exploration and research are at an advanced stage, and while we are hopeful, we must wait for the process of exploration to take its course.

Trade and Foreign Affairs
Fellow Gambians

By exercising your democratic rights last December, you helped us usher in a new Gambia that is more open to the world and a better neighbor within our region. We now have a country that will benefit from greater openness through international tourism.

Since my inauguration, it is clear that the world appreciates the Gambia and wants to engage with us. We have already seen an increase in the volume of cargo at the Port of Banjul as well as rise in vehicular traffic using the ferry services. Furthermore, there has been a clear boost in the flock of new investors exploring opportunities in our country.

We have also been honoured with many visits by foreign dignitaries from the EU, the UN, the UK and from our own ECOWAS neighbours. I have equality been humbled by invitations from fellow world leaders.

The Gambia has begun the process of rejoining the Commonwealth and reaffirmed our membership to the International Criminal Court; we have welcomed the decision by ECOWAS to extend ECOMIG's tenure, all of which demonstrates our commitment to embrace regional and global institutions in the name of open and collaborative international relations.

Relations with our neighbour Senegal have been transformed positively. We now meet as strategic partners who recognize the mutual benefit of closer co-

operation. Within the first 100 days of our period in office, our countries signed several key agreements on defence and security, tourism, fisheries and consular assistance.

As a small economy, The Gambia has much to gain from different trade across our borders with Senegal and beyond. Going forward, my Cabinet and I will work to make the most of these opportunities to boost our economy and create jobs for Gambians. Already, the National Assembly ratified a crucial World Trade Organization (WTO) trade facilitation agreement. This is an agreement that will make The Gambia a more attractive export destination for our trading partners. I am proud to announce that my Minister of Trade has since signed a letter of agreement with China for duty free trade between our two nations.

This will remove the need for costly trans-shipments of Gambian exports to China through a third country. It will also make our goods more competitive, and boost our export potential to the world's largest markets. A legal metrology bill soon be brought to the floor of the National Assembly. The bill will, among other things, address consumer protection relevant to legal metrology functions.

International Financial Affairs and Public Finances

Fellow Gambian, my government took office to discover that the Treasury was virtually empty and domestic and foreign debts at an all –time high. The foreign reserves at the Central bank were less than one month import cover, and the economic and governance situation had becomes so bad that our international development partners had deserted us.

To address this crisis, my government in January 2017 developed the Accelerated National Response Plan which seeks technical and financial support from our development partners to help mitigate the economic and fiscal crisis in the short-term. We are grateful to our international partners, who have respond swiftly and continue to respond to this call for support.

The European Union has made a significant financial and commitment. It is disbursing frozen funds and committing new funds to support the development agenda of the New Gambia. The World Bank has already provided vital emergency budget support and we are in the final stages of concluding a Rapid Credit Facility Agreement with the IMF who have agreed to a staff monitored programme to stabilize the economy and public finances. This will include the reform of public enterprises such as the National Water and Electricity Corporation (NAWEC) and telecommunications entities GAMTEL and GAMCEL.

Youth

In order to take full advantage of the impending financial and economic opportunities, we need to prepare our youth today for a vibrant labour force tomorrow. After all, the bedrock of our country's very existence is our youth. This is why the Ministry of Youth and Sports is tasked to create various capacity and employment initiatives to enable our young people to form the much-needed human capital that will drive the country's development agenda.

In our first 100 days, a new Youth Employment Project initiative supported by the EU was launched at the Ministry of Trade, Industry, Regional Integration and Employment. The objective of this project is to improve the skills of potential youth workers and prepare them, especially returning young migrants for the labour market.

Through the President's International Award Scheme, 60 youths were recently enrolled to undergo skills training in a range of technical and vocational areas like auto-mechanics, carpentry and secretarial work. It is encouraging to note that the National Youth Council coordinates the civic education programme. This is aimed at mobilizing our youth to participate in politics, and to assume their rightful role in the country's development process. The Council has helped craft a young agenda for government's consideration, and is working closely with the International Organization for migration to support returnees and potential migrants to acquire livelihood skills in horticulture and poultry.

The Council is also helping young people in Busumbala, Baddibu Salikenni, and Kuntaur to acquire skills in poultry farming. Similarly, it is helping young people in Wuli to acquire skills in horticulture. These capacity building initiatives also sensitise young people to the dangers of illegal migration to Europe.

Agriculture

In agriculture, we expect to make critical development gains from improving the skills of our youth and encouraging them to participate in agriculture. At the moment, agricultural productivity is low, and this limits the benefits to the nation in terms of jobs, livelihoods and government revenue.

In addition to youth training, the Ministry of Agriculture has begun a programme of support to farmers and farming businesses to improve seed input, modernize cropping and ploughing techniques, and enhance planning in the face of climate change and other hazards to agriculture. Already, vegetable seeds have been distributed to 11,200 farmers as well as 22,500 kilogrammes of rice seeds to intensify rice production. High quality fertilizer and groundnut seeds have also been made available to farmers at subsidized prices.

Fisheries

As well as maximizing the economic potential of our agricultural sub-sector, we have begun to develop fisheries as a source of food security, jobs and economic growth. During the first 100 days of my presidency, the Ministry of Fisheries, Water Resources and National Assembly Matters and the Ministry of Justice reviewed the country's 2008 fisheries regulations to make it more relevant to our current realities.

Considering that our industrial fisheries sector has been dormant for over twenty years, we expect that the amendment of those regulations will contribute to the sustainable conservation and management of the fisheries sector. It will also enhance food security for all Gambians and contribute to poverty reduction through employment creation.

Tourism

Our historic political transition took place during the peak of the tourist season. Tourism contributes significantly to GDP and it is a critical source of employment and government revenue, as tourists are naturally drawn to our warm and friendly shores. We have begun to re-engage our key markets but we still have a lot to do to sell our New Gambia brand to the world. We intend to realize the full potential of tourism as a source of employment, livelihoods and prosperity for our nation.

The implementation of new strategies to enhance culture, tradition and the arts as channels for new tourist inflows is already underway. The major craft markets at Bungalow Beach Hotel and Fajara Hotel have already been upgraded. Community-based tourism endeavours, such as the one in Ndemban in the West Coast Region, have been developed with the support of the Ministry of Tourism and Culture.

Environment and Climate change

In support of environmental protection and tourism in the country, my government has put in place the right policies and programmes to protect our environment and combat the effects of climate change. In our first 100 days, we reversed an executive order of the previous government to destroy the forest park in Bijilo with the construction of a hotel on the park ground. We have normalized the environmental impact assessment process with clear guidelines in accordance with due process, with full transparency, to give investors more confidence in the system.

My government will continue to monitor to ensure that existing investors respect the agreed guiltiness to protect our environment. My government has also mobilized additional resources to supported environmental protection.

We have re-engaged with the Global Environment Facility and we will access US$6 million that had previously been withheld.

The Forestry Bill 2017, which seeks to put in place the necessarily legal framework for the management of our forest resources, will come to this Assembly shortly for enactment. We shall enforce it rigorously to protect and preserve our already degraded and vulnerable forest cover. This is necessary, not only to preserve our precious natural resources, but also to militate against the adverse effects of climate change.

Water

Within the first 100 days of my government, we have made important progress in expanding access to safe drinking water and improved sanitation in rural areas. On the 9th of April, with a grant from the Saudi Fund for Development, my government signed a contract for the construction of 25 drilled wells, equipped with solar pumps. The contract also provides for 25 elevated water tanks, and associated water distribution systems. This US$6 million project will improve water supply in rural areas by providing safe drinking water with easy to operate systems.

In March 2017, the Department of Water Resources completed the construction of 950 ventilated improved pit latrines out of planned 1,000 nationwide. The Ministry is currently installing tanks, laying water pipes and building pre-cast stands in various communities across the country.

Many of these facilities are either complete or nearing completion. At the end of this project, over 65,000 people in rural areas will have access to safe drinking water and 44,000 will have access to improved toilet facilities.

Health

Madam Speaker,

Improvements to water quality are linked to health outcomes across the country. Alongside providing people with safe drinking water and sanitation, my government, through the Ministry of Health, is scaling up its efforts to improve our health delivery systems, especially for women and children. As a first step, we have obtained additional assets to support primary health care provision in the country. This includes 800 pedal bicycles and 29 motorbikes for Village Health Workers and Community Health Nurses across the country's seven health regions.

I am pleased to report that the World Bank has approved US$7 million in additional funding for the Maternal and Child Health as well as the Nutrition Result Project. My government has also submitted a proposal to the EU to *enhance food security. We would welcome their support to help us treat acute malnutrition and prevent all forms of under-nutrition.*

With more than 95 percent coverage, we are also getting support from the Global Alliance for Vaccine Initiative (GAVI) to help us consolidate our strong track record on child immunizations. This project, estimated at US$4.6 million will help strengthen and enhance our immunization systems.

Education

Education for basic and secondary education, I am proud to say we have reached agreement with development partners for over US$50 million worth of investment to expand and improve education for our generation.

With the help of the Kuwait Fund, we are upgrading 39 upper basic and senior secondary schools. This will see the building of additional classrooms, the rehabilitation of existing ones, as well as information technology and solar power solutions. We will install new furniture and educational facilities in our schools, including science laboratories and there will be a new teaching curriculum. With support from the World Bank and the Global Partnership for Education, we are building on existing programmes to enhance access to quality basic education, including early childhood education.

Administrative and Civil Service

Madam Speaker, while initiating our policy and reform agenda, we have also been reforming ourselves within the government. We inherited a highly politicized regional administrative system. It was presided over by governors who owed their allegiance to the APRC.

Officers of regional governors were being run more as political bureaus rather than serving the grassroots within their localities. As such, scare national resources were being used for political propaganda activities. To improve governance and stop wasting resources, my government appointed five new governors whose terms f reference clearly exclude them from engaging in partisan politics. We have encouraged them to follow proper civil service conduct, which embodies neutrality and impartiality in performing their functions.

In normalising the civil service, we have established a panel to review the wrongful dismissal of civil servants and other government officials between September 1997 and December 2016. Since its creation, the panel has cleared over 100 employees, allowing them to be reinstated. At the same time, the civil service has expanded rapidly by over 40 percent since 2007. Consequently, almost half of the government budget is spent on civil service wages and benefits. This not only limits government's ability to provide the necessary budget to improve the socio-economic status of its citizens, but also makes it difficult to improve the salary of civil servants. This is one of the key challenges in attracting and retaining skilled professionals.

In response, my government has tasked the Personnel Management Office to conduct a comprehensive nationwide staff audit for the entire civil service. This began on 27 March, 2017. For the first time, the audit included the security forces-the Army, Police, Immigration, Prisons, Fire and Rescue Service and the State Intelligence Service. The objectives of the audit exercise include the identification and elimination of ghost workers, the recovery of wrongful salaries and the upgrading of personnel records.

Let me proudly acknowledge the support that my government received from our UN partners in the area of administrative reform. During this transition period, the UN system has provided support to strengthen government capacity and they have been assisting us in the formulation of our National Development Plan, as well as security sector reforms. It is important to report that as part of the reforms, my own office which was directly coordinating and supervising a huge number of public enterprises and other state agencies under the former government has been de-congested and those institutions streamlined with their line ministries.

In conclusion

While we have taken this opportunity to reflect on how far we have progress as a nation in just a few short months, let us not be mistaken, we have a huge long-term task ahead. This includes but not limited to:

- Continuing to rebuild and nurture our young democracy for inclusive socio-economic development;
- Providing economic opportunities for all; and
- Reforming the institutions of government to ensure improved service delivery for our people.

These tasks are not without challenges, but I am confident that none of them are impossible to overcome. I am happy and privileged to have the great opportunity to lead our great nation to prosperity. But we must learn from the experience of others. We must be disciplined, follow the plan and stay committed to that plan. So in pursuing our vision for the New Gambia, my government will continue to focus our time and resources on a clear agenda. We shall create a foundation on which future progress will be built.

I commit to you to pursue this agenda with greater transparency and accountability-more than ever before. I will continue to update you on progress throughout the year. This is a new government and a new era, and as your President, I am here to serve the Gambian people. and now, by the powers

vested in me as President, it is my pleasure and privilege to declare this historic session of our National assembly in the new Gambia formally open.
Thank you.

The text of the coalition's one year anniversary reads:
Your Excellency the Vice President,
The Speaker of the National Assembly,
Your Lordship the Chief Justice,
Secretary General & Head of the Civil Service
Cabinet Ministers,
Diplomatic and Consular Corps,
Members of the National Assembly,
Members of the Coalition Executive,
Members of President Barrow National Youth Development Front,
Members of the Media Fraternity,
Distinguished guests, ladies and gentlemen,
All protocol duly observed
I thank the Almighty Allah for making us witness this momentous occasion marking the first anniversary since our beloved country witnessed the ushering in of a new democracy after 22 years of dictatorship.

Today marks a significant day in the annals of our history when the great people of this country came together and won a landmark victory against a brutal dictatorship through a democratic process. On that fateful day one year ago, this nation took a stand and liberated itself from politics of fear, intimidation and division, and embraced hope, diversity and respect for human dignity and the rule of law.

The change has been both dramatic and decisive with the people of the country resolving never again to return to the dark days of mismanagement and unconstitutional rule. Consequently, because of our determination, we are witnessing the beginning of a new and unfolding democracy based on justice, freedom, equality and fraternity.

This glorious and historic victory did not just drop from the sky, there are quite a huge number of courageous individuals, groups and partners both within the country and abroad who contributed greatly to the success of our national struggle for democracy and good governance.

This day therefore is quite befitting for us to assemble in this impressive numbers to once more say thank you to all Gambian women and men; our youth, Gambians in the diaspora, ECOWAS bloc, UN, EU and other development partners and friends of The Gambia who were at the forefront of the struggle to end impunity and dictatorship.

I must also commend the leaders of the political parties for setting aside personal ambitions in favour of national interest by uniting to support my candidacy as the flag bearer following my election at the convention. While we gather to celebrate our great achievement, we must also remember, celebrate and pray for the brave and gallant Gambians who have paid the ultimate price for us to enjoy the freedom, democracy and rule of law that prevails today. They held the beacon of freedom and liberty high in the face of tyranny. We thank God for their sacrifice but let me say this and say it with the utmost conviction: their lives, pains, and struggles shall never go in vain.

We owe them a debt of gratitude and this must be manifested in our efforts to strengthen democracy, human rights and positive development geared towards improving quality of lives for the population irrespective of political affiliation, gender, ethnic or religious considerations. The strength of our nation lies in its unity in diversity.

Ladies and gentlemen,

My government owes you clear policies and practical measures to ensure that everyone particularly the youth and women contribute to and benefit from our new democracy.

This we have started to do; and today I am proud to announce that Our National Development Plan 2018-2021 has now been validated.

This plan has among other things mainstreamed youth development, gender and poverty reduction as well as sound fiscal and macro management policies with the tendency to grow the economy and create decent jobs for our unemployed youths and women.

Fellow Gambians, the challenges are enormous given what this government has inherited. Let me take this opportunity to call on all of you to stand as one and face the task ahead and turn these overwhelming challenges into opportunities in the new dawn. Let us make this the beginning of a genuine recovery and sustainable development for posterity.

One of the critical steps being taken by my administration is the implementation of specific measures to restore confidence in governance.

These measures will help create the right environment required to pull the country back on the path of development and growth. The efforts are in fact well in progress and the new policies and programmes of the government have started to bear fruits.

Since my inauguration as President, we have successfully ended The Gambia's isolation from the rest of the world. There has been a rise in bilateral and multilateral cooperation as partners have regained confidence to engage the government.

This is reflected among other things in the increased economic activities as a result of the conducive business environment created by this government leading to the stability of prices of basic commodities which are in fact generally going down.

It is also important to note that resultant demands on the services of the Banjul Port far exceeds the current capacity thus the government has taken the decision for the port to operate 24 hours creating more employment and improving timely service delivery.

Furthermore, we have as a government reduced the price of fuel three times in less than a year in line with world market prices. This has positive impact on commodity prices and their availability across the country.

Another positive achievement of my Government's ongoing policies is its commitment to fiscal discipline. This is reflected in the remarkable improvement on the country's foreign exchange reserve of well over 4 months import cover in a short space of time, compared to less than one month when we took over government.

Fellow Gambians, I am pleased to inform you that Gambian legal experts continue to be steadily appointed in our Judiciary in line with our efforts to fully "Gambianise" the Bench.

My government values the role of women in development and places gender representation high on the agenda which is proven by the appointment of numerous female Judges at the superior courts.

The pursuit of justice remains a high priority for my government. Some notable achievements include the decongestion of the prisons, the establishment of a Criminal Case and Detention Review Panel, the setting up of a Commission of Inquiry to look into the financial and business-related activities of the former President and his associates. We also held a successful National Stakeholders' Conference on Justice and Human Rights earlier in May. The forum provided a unique opportunity for inclusive dialogue and consultations on key justice sector reforms, including plans for the setting up of the Truth and Reconciliation and Human Rights Commissions.

My government has received and continues to benefit from genuine and solid support provided by the UN in the area of transitional justice.

Tourism continues to be a key priority area of my government as it contributes significantly to our GDP.

It is an important source of employment and government revenue. Government through the Ministry of Tourism is actively engaging stakeholders and partners to continue to improve and diversify the product base of the sector, in the areas of eco-tourism, river cruising, cultural tourism, among others.

The Ministry has recently signed an MOU with a key partner (F. T. I.) who will potentially increase the number of arrivals and help build capacity through the Tourism Institute. These efforts are in line with the overall government policy of making the industry an all-year-round activity.

Ladies and gentlemen, agriculture constitutes the backbone of our economy; and yet the potentials of this critical sector remain largely untapped. It is not by accident that the agricultural sub-sector is among the top five priority areas of my government.

Mechanisation and value addition are central to the achievement of food self -sufficiency. As I have always said, it is the duty and responsibility of all Gambians - you and me - to bring about sustainable national development for our people; others can only help.

In this process, the youths who constitute over 60% of the population must play a crucial role. This is why I am always encouraged when I see talented, dedicated and disciplined youths coming together to advance the course of national development.

Today, I am particularly pleased and privileged to launch this youth group which is named in my honour, willing, able and ready to join hands with other youth organizations across the country in pursuit of national development. Essentially, it is through endeavours like this that we can progressively harness the demographic dividends of our gallant youths.

On this note it is now my honour to formerly launch The President Barrow National Youth Development Front. Let me end this address by once again advising this youth group just launched and those throughout the country as our future leaders to stay disciplined and focused on acquiring knowledge and skills necessary for nation building.

Thank you all for your kind attention.

President Barrow's new year's address reads:
Fellow Gambians

Let me start by thanking almighty Allah (SWT) for making us all witness the end of this eventful year, and beginning of the New Year with high hopes and aspirations for a better future.

As I extend the traditional national New Year greetings of goodwill and prosperity to you, I wish to take this opportunity to share some of the highlights of the passing year. It is also a time for reflections and analysis of the coming year and beyond.

In twenty days' time, it will be exactly one year when I was sworn in as the President of this country following my election on December 1st 2016. The refusal of the former president to accept the outcome of those results, set into motion sequence of events with far reaching political, socio-economic and security implications, which has greatly affected smooth functioning of the state machinery.

Indeed, when you elected me as the president of this beautiful country, it was no mistake that the task ahead of me is not only challenging but also huge and demanding. However, never in my mind have I doubted our great potentials to rebuild our country. We have the human resources comprising of talented youthful population, as well as the geographical advantage to make this great country a force to reckon with in the sub region.

That is my belief and it is anchored on the fact that I have confidence in my administration but more so in you Gambians to collectively transform our economy, deepen our democracy and rule of law.

In the face of a commanding resistance, you must be applauded for taken your country back from the dictatorship that far too long strangled our country, suppressed our potential to grow, dwarf our spirit and confidence to compete on the global stage. This is not just an incredible feat but a clear manifestation that with the collective efforts and sacrifice of Gambians here and abroad, no challenge facing our country is impossible for us to handle.

This is why my administration is working tirelessly to ensure that there in transitional justice, while we undertake the needed processes for institutional, social and political reforms. We must all set our mind that together we can set the standards for a prosperous nation now and for the next generations.

However, it is clear that we did not begin this task with the best of the conditions. We started from a position undermined by decades of mismanagement and undemocratic consolidation of power, that weaken our institutions, our coffers not only emptied, but we are loaded with huge debt. The country has debts of more than 1 billion US dollars which is a staggering 120% of debt to GDP, this is equivalent to each household owing about 4500 US dollars. In addition, state assets have been neglected. Electricity is a case in point.

NAWEC Generators have not been maintained and have been run into the ground. In October two generators were shut down for scheduled overhaul, but in the course of a few weeks three other generators broke down, this caused unacceptable power cuts.

I must say I was deeply encouraged by the level of patience demonstrated by the Gambians under the difficult condition. As a government, we have taken the decision to plan for additional new power plant as a medium and long-term plan and a complete overhaul of the ageing generators. My Government has set out an energy Roadmap to help fix the continuous energy crisis. This plan is already attracting donors and investors.

These are some steps we have undertaken for this country to graduate from isolation and collapse economy to a vibrant destination for investors and a centre of attractions for people in the sub region and beyond.

During the year under review my administration has forged relationship with many development partners and made so many genuine friends within a short span of time. We engaged many partners to rebuild our economy but also our social ties across religious, geographical and political boundaries. This goodwill has since translated into benefits as we see signs of progress in our democracy and macro-economic status. The port has seen an increase in trade. Tourism has recovered and there is a mark improvement in our macro-economic status.

The GDP growth for 2018 is projected at 3.8 percent compared to a growth of 2.2 percent in 2016. The agriculture, industry and service sectors are all expected to register positive growth compare to the year ending.

Inflation has reversed its rising trend declining from 8.8 percent in January to 7.4 percent in October 2017 reflecting the gradual decline in food prices and stabilization of the Dalasi.

Treasury bill rates have declined between September 2016 and September 2017. This has reduced the cost of Government's borrowing by close to 50 percent and this trend is set to continue in the coming year.

The Dalasi has remained stable since April 2017; with gross international reserves increasing from less than one month of import cover at end-2016 to well over 4 months by the end of year under review.

Fellow Gambians and friends of The Gambia,

Given that no country can survive in global isolation more so a small country with limited natural resources like ours, one of the first assignments of my government is to return our country into the fold of the international community. We have already set the ball rolling for re-joining the Commonwealth and other international bodies such as the International Criminal Court and we have also reaffirmed our membership in the international centre for settlement of investment disputes to encourage and restore Investors' confidence.

My administration has already signed the Trade Facilitation Agreement with the World Trade Organization, to ease access to markets and have an improved investment environment.

Fellow Citizens,

We have since restored free speech and freedom of the press. Politics of fear and intimidation have no place in today's Gambia. We usher in an age of dialogue and transparency. My Government also encourages all Gambians to be informed and engaged. This is demonstrated by the increase in youth and women participation in the democratic process. We have encouraged openness to the media to promote dialogue and understanding on our national issues, thus promoting freedom of expression and opinion.

Fellow Gambians,

In the development process, it is practically impossible to take on all development challenges at once, this is why prioritisation and focus is important. In this regard, following careful consideration I have personally identified the following five thematic areas as my presidential priorities during my tenure of office.

- *Energy and Infrastructure,*
- *Agriculture,*
- *Health*
- *Education and Youth Empowerment*
- *Tourism,*

These areas will be monitored with keen interest to ensure that my Government achieves key milestones and targets which are now being worked out at the technical level.

It is also important to note that these presidential priorities have also been incorporated in the National Development Plan as required. This government blueprint which has already been validated is an all-inclusive plan with clear vision and implementation strategies.

In conclusion, as we usher in the New Year, let us make firm resolutions as a country with the bold objective of constructive change and work towards achieving exciting new possibilities in our personal lives, as well as in the life of our nation.

I urge all Gambians and friends of The Gambia to redouble our efforts and dedication to timely and effective implementation of our development plan. This requires sectoral leadership in the ministries, departments and agencies to monitor and supervise the implementation and outcomes of the National Development Plan.

And let us go forward into 2018 with optimism and faith in our ability to achieve and succeed.

I pray to almighty Allah to grant us all a New Year filled with good health, prosperity and happiness.

Thank you.

Obviously The Gambia like many countries around the world has a great concern for the welfare of its youth. It is the reason the government has Ministry of Youth and Sports that is responsible for making policy as well as co-operating with donor agencies for youth development programs. The Ministry has undertaken innovative measures in decentralizing its functions for a more effective implementation of the programmes of its policy objectives. This has brought about a breaking of new ground and major achievements in the field of youth and sports. However, it is very clear that to realize youth empowerment, the developing countries would need to partner with the developed countries in the area of mobilizing the necessary funds to create entrepreneurship development programmes for the youth that would enable them acquire the necessary knowledge and business skills that could be used to help them earn a decent living.

Having entrepreneurial skills will help the youth to take charge of their destiny in their continent and will prevent the mass movement of people across the dangerous desert in the name of searching greener pasture. I urge the World powers to support the developing countries with projects that could transform the lives of many people, particularly the growing youth population majority of who are unemployed.

Also, as more and more youth retuned from Libya, there is a need for the government to act quickly and create employment opportunities. Let everyone understand that many of the returnees came without money. They also found nothing at home because they sold properties and other belongings with the hope of getting to the developed world. As they have failed to realized their dreams there is a need to help them establish themselves quickly. Let the world knows that it would be a terrible mistake to ignore them as that will lead to more poverty and frustration. There are lots of returnees without a job which means the level of poverty will be on the increase if an urgent action is not taken to address their plight. The returnees need to get employment so as to realize the full re-integration. It is important to know that many of these people feels embarrassed for retuning without money. Also there has to be public sensitization to make families understand that retuning home after travel is not aimless rather could be an opportunity for people to fully apply themselves in their home country and contribute in nation building.

6

Studying & Working in the UK

As many youth of africa risked their lives to reach Europe in search of greener pasture, I deem it necessary to share my experiences not for any reason to discourage the youth but to enable them get facts about some of the challenges migrants endure in UK while reading and working so as to pay tuition fees and accommodation . I spoke with lots of migrants who lived in other countries around the world to know their know-hows with regards to challenges they encountered while working and studying in those countries. The move enabled me know that my experiences in UK was nothing different from the experiences these people had in Europe and America. Truly, it is the wishes of many young people particularly those in Africa to live and read in Europe and America. Unfortunately, not everyone realizes their dreams due to many different factors, one of which is the lack of necessary financial support to get visa and pay for air ticket.

It is an open fact that the developed countries has better learning facilities and materials that when one have the chance to utilize properly can help one to acquire new knowledge and skills necessary for the development of oneself and ones country through employment. It was in view of this belief that I among many struggled to look for such an opportunity that could assist me to study in the United Kingdom. Once I got the opportunity, I then prepared for the journey which was proven to be difficult in the beginning than I thought but thank God despite the many challenges encountered on the journey, I was able to make it through to United Kingdom where I read from a diploma programme to a degree after many years of hard work and commitment to studies.

Actually, when I first arrived in the United Kingdom it was like I had already achieved my aim in life. It was only on my second day in London that I wanted to see what was going on in the streets of London. My curiosity led me to my first disappointment when I was told that I needed to take permission from my host before I could go out. To seek permission sounded funny to me because I could not imagine obtaining permission from someone to go out while I was at home in The Gambia. To comply with this directive, I took a few minutes to think about it, and after a while I accepted the move as I reminded myself that I was in a foreign country . As I agreed my host took me to the streets of London, a walk that lasted for just few minutes before we returned to the house for lunch.

Honestly, I spent almost a week indoors watching television before my host accompanied me to South Chelsea College in Brixton for registration. On my first journey to the college, I was told that London is a big city, that to know every place is a problem let alone to visit all. So one very interesting thing I had to do on my first visit to the college was to return home alone using a map of London city. It was a tube that we took from Seven Sisters' Station changed at Victoria before our destination in Brixton. Upon arrival at Brixton tube station, I was provided with a copy of a map which I was not sure whether I could use because I was never a geography student neither was I ever involved in map reading. All the same I realized that this was the UK and I had no choice but to hold a map to guide me through the city of London. Upon arrival at Brixton tube station, we walked to South Chelsea College, where, after following the queue, registered as a student. Obviously, I had all the necessary documentation required from a foreign student in London.

After the registration process, my host asked me to follow him on the corridor where he told me that he was to depart for work and that I should use a map to return to the house in the evening. As he walked through the stairs while I stood looking at him I said to myself that so it is true that only by reading a map could I find my way back to Tottenham in North London? To be honest, I almost lost concentration in the classroom on my first day at college because I had to imagine how to go back to Tottenham after lectures. Nonetheless, when the classes ended for the day I came through the stairs of South Chelsea College and walked to the Brixton tube station where I joined a tube to Seven Sisters' Station at Tottenham as directed by my host. While on board the tube I took out the map from my handbag looked at it thoroughly in order to locate where the tube was as opposed to my destination. As I read the map and sat uncomfortably doubting whether I would be able to get to my destination, I had an announcement informing passengers that the tube was about to depart. Interestingly, as we departed from Brixton and arrived at the first tube station along the way an announcement was made informing passengers about the tube station that we were at the time. As the tube moved the announcement continued at every station that we arrived, a move that gave hope to me that I would not miss my destination at Seven Sisters' Station. Obviously, the announcements made on the tube were one thing that my host forgot to inform me about.

However, I paid great attention to the announcements made and before I knew the tube arrived at Seven Sisters' Station. I came out of the tube station and walked for a distance to the house at Tottenham. Upon my arrival at the house, I pressed the bell and waited for my host to open the door for me to enter. As I walked through the door to the sitting room, where my host was seated eagerly waiting to know how I was able to return home, I took my time to explain the story as he listened carefully and at the end of my narration he apologized for forgetting to inform me that there are announcements made on the tube at every station.

However, it took me three weeks before I could get employed in London as a casual worker at a busy restaurant located at Liverpool Street in London. At that restaurant I usually worked from 10 pm to 7 am Monday to Friday and in the morning I travelled from Liverpool Street usually by bus to Victoria where I changed for another bus to Brixton to attend lectures at South Chelsea College. I had to work at night to be able to make ends meet and to attend full day lectures at the college. From night work I usually arrived at South Chelsea College earlier than most of my colleagues because once I closed at 7 am; I just proceeded to college without going back to Tottenham, which is far from Brixton by bus.

Important information that many foreign students will tell one about student life in London includes lack of enough time to sleep and so I went through the same thing. There was not enough time with me to sleep, since I closed from work at 7 am and attended lectures at 10 am in Brixton. In a nutshell, I had three hours interval from work to class and there was a huge distance to cover. All that I could do like many students, was to have some sleep on the train, tube or bus depending on which one that I used. Again to sleep on the journey could be horrible for many people since many of us usually missed our destination while sleeping and could only realize this when the bus or train got to the termination end. .

This was the kind of life that many students lived on in London and so I am not an exception. I spent two years at South Chelsea College from a certificate and then IT diploma programme . Interestingly, many foreign students in those days were tested on their performance before they could be enrolled in the right classroom and so I also experienced the same. It was very clear from my school papers that I obtained a diploma in IT from The Gambia Technical Training Institute before travelling to London, but at South Chelsea College I had to start again from a certificate level to a Diploma.

As I complied with this rule, my lecturers soon found out that I was helping other students any time an assignment was given. At the end of the diploma programme I had an impressive result, one that nearly caused my ambition to change college from South Chelsea to City Banking College in London as I was requested to stay after I had made my intention known. I insisted that I had to leave and so I applied for a Diploma Programme at City Banking College in central London. The programme at City Banking College was a Postgraduate Diploma in Banking and Finance. My application was successful and then I started the Post graduate Diploma Programme in Banking and Financial Services at City Banking College. While on the programme I decided to look for another job different from working at the restaurant in Liverpool Street, London.

My job search lasted for almost three months during which lectures progressed at City Banking College. At the end of the three-month period, I got employed as a retail security officer posted at various Tesco shops in London and outside. When I took up the new security job, I realized that the job paid higher than the restaurant work. After six months on the job, I found out that I had travelled far and wide in London and outside where I met new friends. In addition to that, the job made me known to many of my fellow countrymen as they came to find out about the company that I worked for. The job also assisted me to do a lot in the Gambia, especially on my building construction. I used part of the proceeds from my security job to build a solid house where I live with my family. Thank God this was made possible through hard work that I went through as a security officer in London. It is interesting to know that to be an ordinary security officer in most African countries is considered a dormant job when many migrants in the West look for a security job because it is highly paid. I have the belief that many migrants can confirm that it was difficult to get a security job in London.

In my case, when I saw an advert for the position of a security officer in the newspapers in London, I sent in my application to the company. After a week I was called and invited for an interview. On the day set aside for the interview, I woke up early and went to the company. The interview was held at 10:30 am and three days later those that attended the interview were once again invited to the manager's office. When we arrived, we were taken to a camera room where the manager played a video cassette showing the different types of crimes and offence committed by bandits or thieves, mainly in shops and factories. The video lasted for twenty minutes, after which each of us were provided with questions and answer sheets that contained exactly what we watched on the video. It was a half- anhour examination for not more than forty-five questions to answer. When we finished answering the questions, the results were made known to us on that very day.

When the results were released, I came second from the five of us. But as I waited for the results for the other members I was shocked to know that one fellow that I stood outside with discussing before the exam was said to have failed the exam. I was sad because when I was worried about whether I would be able to make it, he was there to give me courage. In fact even when I reached the house in Tottenham, I had to sit in the sitting room meditating about the nice fellow. However for those of us who had good results from the examination we were on a later date called to collect our appointment letters for the position of a security officer. Even as a security officer, I continued to work at night because as a student in the UK I thought it was wise to work at night and attend lectures in the morning than to choose two or three working days during daytime. So I served as a security officer for two years, with lots of travel and training sessions to attend. Over time, I also moved from Tottenham to Newington when I found a room cheaper than that of Tottenham. But again after four months, I came back to Tottenham and at the time was to stay with other Gambians that I met later in London.

One thing that I found common during my stay in London was that most migrants often changed their addresses only to look for somewhere affordable to rent. It is an open fact that many migrants depended on casual jobs in London and most of those jobs paid little that could not meet one's needs in London not to talk about fulfilling one's commitments back home.

Student life in London could be seen as a period of intense struggle with little time for oneself, let alone for anyone to chat with apart from workplaces and classroom. To live in such terrible condition often made many homesick. As a student in the UK one has to work hard, and because of that I took advantage of being a security officer and worked hard to raise more money so as to be able to take care of myself. By doing that, I constantly reminded myself about my reason for being in London, which was to acquire knowledge and so I also paid great attention to my lectures. In order to be able to read I acted as a curious student and registered with many libraries at different locations in London. Those libraries include Tottenham, Stratford, Newington, Edmonton Green and Liverpool Street.

While I was in my final year as a student in London, I decided to reduce the number of my working hours in order to concentrate more on reading and to visit libraries, especially the one at the heart of Liverpool Street where one finds many financial materials to read. My decision at the time assisted me greatly as I was able to perform well in the examination. I believe that in order to be a good student one needs to try and visit a library at least twice a week. The move helped me acquire the necessary knowledge that assisted me greatly, especially in my final examination at University of Leicester.

In order to study in London and be able to visit many libraries you need to have a valid bus, train or London tube fare with you on your entire journey. Obviously, it is unlawful to travel by bus, train or tube without a fare or valid travel pass in London just as in any other country. And as a student in the UK one should desist from traveling without a fare. This may be one of the reasons why migrants need to have some funds in their account at all times. It is true that not everyone is far from a library in London; some are lucky to reside somewhere close to a library and therefore need no fare to get to the library but even then one may need a travel fare to work. However, it is important for one to have a fare at all times.

Most libraries in London open for long hours and can be accessed by people of different categories, including the young and the aged who are sometimes there to read newspapers and other magazines. As you enter through the library you are required to keep silence and avoid distracting readers with phone calls and unnecessary talk. In fact at times when I was less busy in the library I took a good look at the aged thinking what their age mates in Africa would be doing. However, even life for the aged in London is different from that of the ones in most African countries; they are better informed, more current to happenings but lack social interaction. It is true that there are many other materials in London libraries including CDs and other educative cassettes, and a children's wing where children have access to different useful materials. Another thing that I liked during my visits to libraries in London was the services provided by the librarians. These people are not just workaholics but are keen to respond to any inquiries. If there was anything that contributed to my visits to the library, it was the services that I enjoyed from the librarians.

To read in libraries provided me with accurate mind preparations and so I was seen as a good student in the classroom, especially when I was reading my Master's Degree programme in Business Administration. Any time that I thought about the number of times I visited libraries in London; it reminded me of student life in London. At times I thought of my school bag, which I carried along with me anywhere that I visited. At times to carry a bag in London did not only mean carrying books but it could be a work uniform, where one was required to put on when one finished classes and was to go to work. However this was a period of loneliness, intense struggle and commitment to duty. As I continued with such life, I regained my lost hope after seeing a member of my ghetto boys in London while I was in my third year.

It was a real moment of true reflection on what we missed together back home in The Gambia. It was also a moment to thank God for making it possible for us to see. I   used the opportunity to inform my colleague about my desire to return home after my education as promised while at home in The Gambia. I also told him that I maintained the belief that no matter what I had or wherever I will return to the Gambia by which time my conditions would have changed for good. In fact while I was narrating my experience in London, I decided to keep away some secrets from my colleague and that was to avoid making him discouraged about what he would face in London. Being in London was a lifetime experiences for me as a migrant. For my colleagues in the Gambia, any time they asked to know how was the UK I was quick to respond "very fine and nice place to be", even though it could be horrible for anyone if things fall apart.

Like many migrants I had experienced several difficulties with transportation to school and workplace. It was only when I moved to City Banking College, that some difficulties in travelling were minimized because I could join 149 bus direct from Tottenham to London Bridge and walk to the college. The worst mistake anyone could make in London is to be frequently late either in college or at work. The process involves a real struggle that for one to know, one needs to have the opportunity to go through. Naturally, education is all about mind preparedness but to get educated in London also requires some kind of physical and mental preparedness. For those aspiring to go through the process of education abroad, start to think on how to limit your sleep, idleness, too much visiting or chatting . This may sound funny but before you know it there is no time to waste while you are out there and very little or no time for endless conversations since everyone would be busy doing something. It is a place where one can imagine it to be the best on the earth and that is when things favour you but can always turn against one, especially when one is unlucky to faced job cuts or number of hours cuts and where one has to pay one's rent, take care of one's feeding, travel fares, tuition fees and other commitments back home.

In my own case, I heard lots from people that many tenants in the UK paid rent to their landlords at the end of every week and that was because one was paid every week. However I gave little or no regard to such information until I had to face the reality. To pay rent every week was not the issue but how much one was paid, out of which one had to settle one's rent. In many cases, when one talks about such issues the first thing many would think of is a job to get paid for. Obviously, there are different types of jobs in London just like in other countries but the question is whether desperate migrants can make a choice of jobs? Many migrants entering in the UK have to go through some procedure in order to obtain certain documents like the National Insurance Number (NIN) that helps one to get employed somewhere.

To get some of these documents is not just easy and can involve lots of go-ing and coming with a series of questions, some of which are aimed at estab-lishing one's status in London. Unfortunately, during those difficult times one thinks of one's rent, which has to be paid at the end of the week. It is also an open fact that many landlords in London are not prepared to listen to stories from their tenants but money. Along the way, one gets to know their position, after knowing that most of them have their properties through bank mortgages. It then becomes an issue for every new entrant in the UK to find out how to get a job, which is a good move. However, one can only be given direction to try and not a guarantee that a job can be obtained through a mere job search. There are many ways to go about a job search in London, which include pay-ing a visit to numerous job centres across the city of London. Again to do this one has to have a valid fare for one's journey to and from one job centre to another. During my stay in London I knew that for one to have a job through the job centre, one was required to have a valid passport with a valid visa that is if one is from a visa issuing country, the National Insurance Number (NIN), and tenancy agreement from one's landlord.

Apart from the job centres there were other employment agencies like Adec-co which has one of their offices stationed at Liverpool Street in London. Oth-ers may use the internet search, but, to be honest, for a newcomer it may be advisable to pay a visit to the employment centres than to browse the internet as your first point of contact with an employer. It was a real challenge for us the students in the UK to take up a part-time job which was a requirement in the UK law because most casual jobs for us were not paying much. It then became necessary for one to be much more prepared for a stay in London, especially with one's desire to get educated. In doing so most students in Lon-don struggled through sleepless nights to raise some funds from the number of hours they worked for the purposes of paying their tuition fees. One thing that every student avoided in London was to get late to college as well as work-places. So it was a question of doing things simultaneously for a living.

I want to believe that only a few foreign students in the UK live on scholar-ship. The majority lived to work and pay their tuition fees and rent. Most for-eign students live from hand to mouth; yet their families in their native coun-tries have more expectation from them in terms of financial assistance. To get bored with lots of stress and loneliness' in a foreign land is one side of the coin, wait until when one starts to make numerous phone calls back home and only receives information such as: no food, tuition fees for children, and mon-ey to buy medicine or clothes .Generally if there is money all human beings need to have basic facilities to live, but the issue is whether one is in the situation to afford those facilities.

In fact, few among the foreign students abroad live to wear nice and expensive clothes not to talk about buying expensive cars to drive. I believe a wise student is someone who always has at the back of his mind that he came to a foreign land to get educated and would return home for a better life. Whether such dream are fulfilled or not is one thing but the thinking should be there to guide one through. To be honest, I had the same thought while in London and such thinking guided me to a level that I maintained a low profile. I still imagine how I used to walk in the streets of London, wearing jeans and a jacket with my handbag on my shoulder. I enjoyed such strolls especially when I was going to Tottenham library near Seven Sisters' Station. It is the wish of most migrants in a foreign land to make calls to their countries and talk to their loved ones on a daily basis but such wishes did not often materialize especially when one encountered more requests with limited resources. Such situations often forced others to decide on whether to call home or not. However, such decisions may not be considered appropriate by many but when the going gets tougher others feel that such decisions can help to alleviate one's stress for a period. Almost all the migrants go through such difficulties of stress and I was not an exception. But one thing I was able to maintain despite the numerous demands was to call home at least twice in a week. Any time someone requested for more than what I could do, I tried to do what I could rather than to make myself stressed for someone's problem that was even impossible to justify.

It was good to remember that I was in a foreign country where I needed to have an account and to keep some money with me. It was not difficult to open an account in the UK all that one needed was a valid passport, a letter from an employer if one was working and a tenancy agreement. The procedure was unlike the case in most of countries in Africa where one needs to open an account with some amount of money, in addition to the numerous paper works.

7

Challenges with the Decision to Return Home from Europe

I believe it is beautiful to travel and to return home at some point in time. When one travels for some time and returns home, especially when one is returning from studying abroad, one will be expected to share one's knowledge, skills and experience, especially with those who are not fortunate to have such a chance. It was in line with this belief that I took a decision at the end of my degree programme in London to return home. I believe I made the best decision even though such a decision was considered strange and difficult by other people around me at the time. These people almost saw returning home from Europe as a bad decision even though they were aware that I went to Europe to learn. Actually, the way I was viewed was not different from anyone that lived in Europe and decided to return back in the Gambia. This was because people thought once you lived in Europe you should not return to settle back in the Gambia a thought I was always against because of my understanding of the need to contribute to the development of the Gambia.

It is natural that when one lives abroad for so many years one will be expected to have a good memory on events and happenings that occurred during the time. It is equally important for one to always remember that one left one's country for a purpose and perhaps missed some of one's childhood friends who would be happy to see one returning home with some changes and improvements in one's way of life. Not everyone that misses you will think of seeing you with lots of money but instead attitudinal change and better understanding, especially on how one views the world. One thing that I was mindful of was to avoid calling home to inform my family members and friends that I was coming back home after studies. This was because many people had perceptions that, once one lives in Europe; one does not have to come back home to settle, a belief that does not merge with my thought. And so I came without informing anyone of my plans. In fact, I heard times without number that returnees from study abroad often experience what is known as "re-entry". It is sometimes referred to as re-entry culture shock or return culture shock. Generally, coming home from abroad can be challenging and difficult but can also be the period in which one can learn a lot from one's cultural experience. Re-entry can be the often unexpected and even difficult experience where one needs to re-adjust to one's home culture after missing home for quite a long time.

It is natural that some returnees do not find re-entry difficult, but most of them experience some degree of stress upon their return home. I have met people who told me that the process of re-adapting to their home after their study abroad was more difficult than when they were to adjust to the host culture. Re-entry can be different for everyone, just as everyone's experience abroad was different from others. Some returnees however have some similar re-adjustment issues as they arrive home:

1. Their personal growth and change. One could have experienced some degree of challenge to one's belief, values and the way one views the world after living in a different culture for a while. It is also true that one could have more academic freedom in terms of the way and manner that one went about acquiring education and personal independence during one's stay abroad. At some point one can feel that one is more mature and self-confident after studies abroad. The truth is that after one has spent many years learning abroad one will be expected to change for good.

2. To acquire knowledge and skills, once there is an attitudinal change in one after many years of studying abroad, people will expect one to develop new knowledge, skills and even behaviour patterns. To give an example, one may have developed certain competencies that can assist one to live in one's everyday life abroad such as reading to find out about one's way around a new city so as to act in an appropriate manner, and learn about new things. In addition, one can have competencies that may include new knowledge about one's major, new research skills, and problem -solving skills. A returnee can feel really frustrated after realizing that these skills have little use in their country.

3. How to deal with family and friends. Some returnees are faced with the challenge and difficult issue of how to deal with relationships with their family and friends. Obviously, if one decided to change completely one

would be affected with the way and manner that one wished to deal with his/her family and friends. Some returnees told me that they feel alienation, while other complained of pressure from family and friends thinking that the returnee should revert to the person they were before their travel. To me the most difficult and common is about constantly telling people about one's experience abroad. Many families and friends are often not interested to hear about one's experience abroad.

Well, it was my wish to see many of my colleagues in Europe studying; it is unfortunate that did not happen at the time when I left. However, when I returned to The Gambia, I met many members of the colleagues doing something meaningful for a living. It only took me a few days before I could join the boys in the ghetto despite the fact that many would expect that I should do away with the ghetto boys now that I returned from Europe. I actually came with some new attitudes but not the desire to desert them for who they were and certainly not to forget that I was part of them. It was only when I started to go to the ghetto that I discovered some changes in the way we used to get together and this was because of the different engagements of my colleagues.

One thing that impressed me about my colleagues was that they made themselves available to the ghetto any time they got less busy or when their services were required by any member of the ghetto. We were in a ghetto whose seating usually began at 5:30 pm and ended at around 7:30 pm by which time most of us left for home. The ghetto was viewed by many as a place to exchange ideas and not a room for crime or other illegal acts and certainly not a place to be involved in girls' business. The beauty about the ghetto is that most of us are married and   sometimes one or two of our colleagues' wives comes and sits with us. Just as everyone else picked up a job for themselves in the ghetto, upon my return from London with a degree I applied for a job in many workplaces like banks, insurance companies, within and around the Greater Banjul Area. However it was not easy for me to pick up my first employment as I thought in the beginning in spite of my degree. It is true that I turned down some offers during my job search after I realized that there might be little or no career development in those positions.

When I completed my university degree, I was prepared to pick up any job for a start but along the way in the job search I discovered that some jobs are not good enough to do. As a school leaver one would expect a job in which one could be provided with the necessary training on the job. I only came to realize this during my job search and so I took my time to search for a good job. My job search took me for several months before I could find one. My employment came about after I walked to the Personnel Management Office (PMO) on one fine morning to look for a job. At PMO I walked through the stairs to the secretary's office; who I assumed to be the chairman's secretary and asked if there was any vacancy to apply for.

While I waited for between two and three minutes, the secretary asked me to walk through the stairs down to the notice board and look for job vacancies. I did exactly that and on the notice board I found the advert of four different jobs at various departments within the central government. I stood to look at these jobs for a while before I chose two positions "Customs Officer and the other one was at the Ministry of Finance". On my way back to the secretary's office, I decided that it would be important to ask for advice on the jobs. At the secretary's office, I asked for advice but was told to pick up the application form and see the chairman of the Public Service Commission at his office.

I stood at the chairman's office door and knocked on the door after which I heard a voice that asked me to go in. I pushed the door and entered politely with a smile but I had a mixed feeling as to whether I was going to hear good news or not. I had to think that way because I knew that I was only looking for a chance but had no idea about the jobs that I chose. Anyway in the office I shook hands with the chairman, after which I was offered a seat. I introduced myself to the humble old man who happened to be the late Mr. Njie. As I finished the introduction, the chairman asked about my educational background and the information was provided to him as fast as I could. He then asked for copies of my qualification, which I provided to him without delay. He took a few minutes to go through my qualifications before he could, advise me to apply for the position of Customs Officer. I believe he had reasons for that but I never asked to find out, instead I decided to act on his advice for my own good.

I walked out of the chairman's office after the conversation and I said to myself that the old man had treated me so well that I needed not to forget him. The next move that I took was to go to the secretary's office and inform her that I met the chairman who advised me on what to do.

When I finished with the secretary I walked along the McCarthy Square to the Serekunda / Tabokoto garage in Banjul where I joined the Commercial mini bus from the capital city of Banjul to Churchill's Town in Serekunda. As the vehicle arrived at Churchill's Town, I came out of the car, and walked to the office of the Gambia Telecommunications Company (GAMTEL) at Churchill's Town where I had access to a computer. At GAMTEL I paid twelve dalasi which was the charges for anyone to have access to the computers for thirty minutes in those days and I used the computer to type my CV and the application letter. After typing the application letter and my CV, I left for home only to get prepared for submission the following day. When I woke up the following morning, I went back to the Personnel Management Office in Banjul where I submitted my application for the position of a Customs Officer.

To be precise, I spent almost three months searching for a job, but my search got to an end as I submitted my application to the Personnel Management Office. However, during the three months of job search I was faced with lots of criticisms such as I was deported and could not return to London. Though I was not moved by those comments, until when a situation arose where I discovered that I needed to get employed because my savings at the bank were reducing gradually at the time. Obviously, it would be difficult for me to approach anyone for financial help at the time after living in Europe for so long and with the rumour that was going around that I might have been deported. It was also during that period that I decided to find out about those who truly liked me. In doing so, I saw lots of funny things such as seeing people who have benefited from the little money that I sent to them while I was in Europe turning to hate me. It was a period of real challenge in my life and I knew such a situation could only be overcome with courage and resistance that I needed to keep moving. At no point did I confront anyone for making such false comments but instead I had more courage to look for a job to earn a living and to be able to take care of my family.

It was a difficult moment in which I knew how women are good at fighting back anyone who would want to criticize their relatives. I got to believe this saying when my sister paid numerous visits to my house to ask if I was deported or it was my decision to return home after my degree programme. I was convinced that she was disturbed by comments from some people and perhaps wanted to know the truth before attacking anyone. To make her relax, I told her the truth that I was not deported but only came back with my degree to look for a job and to contribute my quota in national development. However, it was difficult for my sister to accept my story despite my explanation and that was because she heard so many rumours about the issue. In the end, I was able to make her relax and be in a worry free situation.

As I continued with my life while I waited to get a job, I noticed that my loved ones were worried not to see my downfall. It was a period of continuous prayers and in the end God answered the prayers as I was on a sultry afternoon called by the Personnel Management Office and informed that I was short listed for the position of customs officer. The caller also informed me about the interview day, time and venue before putting the phone down. At that point, I got the information that the interview would be held at the Personnel Management Office, the Quadrangle, in Banjul.

When I woke up on the day set aside for the job interview I walked towards the road where I boarded a commercial van at around 8:00 am and arrived in

Banjul at 8: 25 am. The interview was to start at 10:00 am but I thought it was wise to arrive at the PMO One hour thirty minutes before the job interview. Upon my arrival, I walked through the stairs to the waiting room where I sat for almost 45 minutes before taking a decision to look for breakfast. I returned to the Personnel Management Office at 9:30 am after breakfast. I witnessed the coming of many customs officers in uniform. As I sat down to watch these officers, I noticed that each time their fellow uniform man arrived others would greet him with a salute.

To be honest that was when I started to develop mixed feelings on whether I was in the right place at the time. I knew the position was for customs and here were customs officers who I thought were at the PMO for the same job. Then for a moment I felt that if I had to go through the same interview with the officers, I would be the loser in the end, since I had no work experience as a customs officer. Despite my mixed feelings, I sat down with the customs officers on a bench outside the interview room. While we waited for the interview to take place, one of the customs officers came closer to me and greeted me politely. During the chat, he asked lots of questions about me including my qualifications. At first I thought it would not be a good idea to tell him about my qualification because we were about to begin a race which each one would want to keep away from others what they could do. But when he again asked that was the time I told him that I had a degree in business administration. I was also quick to tell him that I did not believe I would get the job of a customs officer after seeing them around for the same position.

What doubted me was that when I completed explaining my worry, the officer smiled before he could surprise me as he acted like blowing a whistle for the information he heard about my qualification. I asked what was the point and the officer told me that they could be in the queue only to accompany me, a comment that sounded funny to me. And I asked what he meant by accompanying me his response was that none of them in the queue had a degree and so I could be lucky to get the job. I never took his comments seriously despite having heard that none of them had a degree. However, as I continued to chat with the officer I noticed that the interview began and that the queue started moving. It was a little while later that his turn came. When he came out from the interview room he looked at me and smiled before I took a good look at him as he walked through the stairs. I did that, thinking that I might not see him again, especially if I failed the interview. Then came my turn and a caller asked me to go inside the interview room where I met the interview panel for the first time in my home country. I comported myself to a level that I could face any challenges. When I was offered a seat, one fellow asked me to introduce myself to the panel, which I did quickly. This was followed by an interview proper where a series of questions were asked by different members of the interview panel.

The interview lasted for some minutes after which I quietly left the Personnel Management Office for home. When I arrived at home, I sat on my bed to think about two things: one was what the customs officer told me and the other one was what would be the result of the interview. I was interrupted when my wife entered to find out how the interview went about and I gave a response that it was not easy but we should have faith in God. Three days later I went to other offices in Banjul where I submitted my other application letters to make a follow-up, because I thought that I should not put all my hopes in one job. That was not a good trip for me since I returned from Banjul with no good news of getting a job. So in the evening I went to the ghetto to chat with friends having in mind that once I attended the ghetto I could easily put the stress aside.

While I continued to associate with the ghetto boys, on one fine Monday, I received a call from the Personnel Management Office during which I was informed that my application for the position of a customs officer was successful. The caller asked me to collect my appointment letter from the Personnel Management Office. At first I assumed the information to be false, but without wasting time, I went to the PMO the very day to collect my appointment letter. When I arrived at the office, I met the secretary who I remembered was the one that had shown me where the notice board was during my job search. She gave me a warm welcome with a smile before she said congratulations to me. The appointment letter was then picked up from the table and given to me, but it was funny for the secretary to hear from me that I did not know where the customs office was. She asked if I as a Gambian never knew where that office was and I responded that I did not know where the customs office is in Banjul.

I was happy that the secretary understood my position and assisted me with the direction to the customs headquarters in Banjul where I was expected to meet the late Director General of Customs at the time, late Mr. Momodou Kabba Tambajang. It was not easy for me to locate customs as I came through the Albert Market in Banjul and asked people on the way, some of whom had no idea about where customs headquarters' was. My finding became easy when I saw the GAMPOST headquarters near the Albert Market. At that point, I remembered that the secretary had mentioned GAMPOST to me in her explanation. As I stood at GAMPOST headquarters waiting to ask someone, I saw one fellow who, after having a word with him, accompanied me to the customs headquarters where we met a Customs guard that I asked for about the Director General of Customs. I guess it was part of their normal security procedure to ask anyone the purpose of their visit and so I went through the same process.

The Customs guard directed me to the Director General's office after he was pleased with my explanation. Upon my arrival at the Director General's office door I politely knocked before being invited in. When I entered and greeted the Director General, he offered me a seat which was placed adjacent to his seat. It took me not more than a minute to introduce myself after which I was assured by the Director General that he had received the information that I was to come. I was not surprised to hear that because I knew he attended our interview at the Personnel Management Office. The humble man did not waste time to accord me a warm welcome after which he advised me to see myself as a member of a big family working towards the interest of The Gambia. It was a short conversation though but very productive in that I received good words that would stay with me so long as I remain alive and work with the government of the Gambia.

It was also a short day for me at work since I was allowed to return home earlier but only to prepare for all day at work the following day. At home I told my wife that I was appointed finally as a Customs officer and that I was to begin the job the following day. At that point, I noticed a kind of happiness in my wife that was never manifested since my return from abroad. All the same, I knew she would be as happy as I was, taking into account what was in the rumour about my decision to return to The Gambia after acquiring my degree in London. In the evening I went to the ghetto where I told my colleagues that I was appointed as a Customs officer. It was a big surprise for me to hear the boys shouting "Customs", good job, and I sat back watching at them for a minute before I asked what the entire shout was for. The response I got was that Customs was one of the best departments that one can work with in The Gambia. I asked why one should think like that and a colleague said to me that most people want to work as Customs officers because it is a noble job especially for those who carry it with the interest of the people and the country at heart. I was also told that Customs deals with revenue collection and that revenue collection was done since at the time of Prophet Muhammad (SAW).

As the chat progressed, more questions were asked by the boys who wanted to know how I went about getting a job at Customs. It was interesting that with the number of times we stayed together, only one among them knew that I had a degree. It was not until I said I got the job through God and that my degree helped. They asked "Degree in what"? I responded quickly as I told them that I had a degree in business administration. There was silence for a while before we continued the chat in the ghetto which was centred on my degree and the new job up to the time that I left the ghetto at 7:3o pm for home.

At home it was time to prepare for work the following day. I opened my cupboard and took out what I believed was one of the best clothes with me at the time. I placed the clothes somewhere that they could easily be reached in the morning. Then I came out to the sitting room where I watched the 10: 00 pm news broadcast on The Gambia Radio and Television Services (GRTS). After the news, I had my dinner, performed the last daily prayer for the day before going to bed in order to wake up early in the morning. Again like most people who are newly employed, I was so happy that to sleep well at night was difficult, because I was eager to start a job after so many months of job search. When I woke up at around 6: 30 am, I took my bath and performed my morning prayers after which I dressed-up and left home at 7: 00 am to the road where I boarded a gele-gele to Banjul. It was my first day to begin a job in my country and I had the belief that my first impression would go a long way. Thank God that I arrived at the Customs office half- an- hour before the official work time which was 8: 00 am. At Customs I sat at one place with a novel in my hand that I read while waiting to see other people to come.

Then at 10:00 o'clock on that fateful morning, I was called to the Director General's office for a brief meeting. Upon my arrival at the office, I found some people that I later found out were the top officers of the department. At the meeting, the Director General told his top officers that I was a new employee in the department and that he wanted them to meet me first before I could be taken around to meet other staff in their different offices. When he finished, other senior officers welcomed me to the department and assured me of their support in the job. At the end of the briefing, I thanked the Director General and his top officers for their warm welcome. I also used the occasion to inform them that I was ready to work cordially with everyone. After that the Director General asked one of the top officers' to accompany me to the office where I was to be for that period. In fact I heard the word "please accompany him to Jerguing", but I did not know what he meant by Jerquing. However, as we arrived at where was referred to as Jerguing, the top officer spoke with the officer in charge of that Unit for some time, after which I was asked to take a seat in an open space where I saw lots of files arranged on cupboards.

As I remained seated, I noticed the movement of different people, some in uniform and others carrying documents and so I suspected that I could have been attached to a busy place. My imagination was soon over when an officer sat near me and asked for my name and purpose of the visit. I responded that I was a new appointee to the department and was told to sit where we were. The officer then welcomed me after which I asked what the word "Jerquing" meant. It was from his response that I knew I was posted to the Internal Audit Unit of Customs referred to as "Jerquing".

On my second day at work, the head of Jerquing invited me in the office and told me that I would be supplied with a uniform and that I should go and meet the department's procurement officer. When I walked out of his office, I started to imagine myself wearing a uniform even though I knew that along the way I would be required to do that as a Customs officer. I was interested to hear the phrase "wearing a uniform" because seeing someone in service uniform was one of the things that I hated to see after the 1981 failed coup led by late Kukoi Samba Sanyang, in the Gambia. To see someone in service uniform in those days often took my memories back to 1981 when I was shocked to see the Senegalese soldiers that walked into my father's shop in Jarra Sikunda where they removed things in the name of searching for weapons. At the time, I asked myself as to what a shopkeeper in the village would want do with the so -called overthrow of the government.

Anyway, I had to change my feelings about the uniform, because I had to wear a uniform as a Customs officer. However, much was yet to happen until when I was issued with a uniform and started to wear it to work. In fact the very first day that I wore a uniform, I had to pass-by our ghetto after work purposely to find out whether I would be viewed differently by my colleagues who were non uniform persons. To my surprise when I arrived in uniform, I noticed some similes and strange looks from my colleagues just as I did to myself. But after a minute the boys told me that I looked good in uniform, a comment that gave me courage that even though I started to wear a uniform my colleagues at the ghetto would still be viewed as usual.

On my second week in the job, I realized that much was to happen when the procurement officer brought gold "epaulettes" for me to put on my uniform, precisely on the shoulder as my rank in the job. I was interested to see a first salute to me immediately after I had completed putting the epaulettes. As I walked out of the office where I was issued my rank and walked through the stairs to the Jerquing section I was greeted with more salutes. While on upstairs I asked the officer that I had an initial chat with to tell me what the epaulettes on my shoulder signified. It was from his explanation that I came to know that I was one of the Senior Officers of the Customs department and so I thanked God who made it possible for granting me the opportunity to have a degree that helped me a better job.

When I closed from work on that day, I passed by our ghetto with my new rank where I was greeted by the boys with happiness. That move made me feel much more comfortable to use the uniform. After a while, I left the ghetto for home where I was welcomed by my family members, some of whom were excited to see me with a rank. I could tell from where I stood that my brothers were discussing my rank and I said to myself that they were excited. It was during this period that I begin to have mush belief in my saying the "hard work pays" which was associated with the belief that my conditions would be better after the return from studies in Europe. However, at Customs Jerquing (Internal Audit Unit) I worked tirelessly with willingness to take up any kind of work that was in line with the process and procedures of the Customs & Excise Department. While doing that I never knew that management took notice of my dedication to duty. After one year at Jerquing, I was posted to Customs Administration as Administrator reporting to the then Deputy Director of Administration. At administration I did everything that I could to bring credit to the department and was loyal to myself, the head of the Customs & Excise Department and The Gambia.

It was out of hard work, dedication and commitment to duty in the administration that after two years I was promoted to the rank of Collector of Customs, carrying two gold epaulettes on each of my shoulders. As I continued to work hard, two years later after the merger between the Departments of Customs & Excise and the Income Tax Department, I was promoted to the rank of a Principal Collector of Customs carrying three gold epaulettes on my shoulder. It happened at a time when the conditions of most of our ghetto boys improved in their various workplaces.

As work at Customs progressed, the Gambia government's decision to merge the then Central Revenue Department with the Customs & Excise Department for better revenue collections kick- started following the appointment of the first Commissioner General in 2006. As the implementation processed progress, the Authority created several positions for suitable candidates to apply. It was followed by the successful recruitment that saw many former staff of the Customs & Excise Department and the then Central Revenue Department employed under the Gambia Revenue Authority. The first position I had under the merger was Appeals Officer at the Customs and Excise Department. The position was actually advertised and I applied before be given the position. I served in that position just for few months before the creation of the Human Resource and Admin-Manager position at the Gambia Revenue Authority.

Actually, when the advert for the position of Human Resource and Admin Manager was released in the local newspapers, many interested applicants sent in their applications. I was never interested to apply for the position until such a time that many believe I could handle the position. It took me a couple of days to think about the decision to apply for the position. While thinking about it I noticed that people around me at the time would not let me rest and so I did what they wanted me to do. After waiting for some time I was on one beautiful day called and informed that, I had been short listed for the position of Human Resource and Admin Manager and that a day was set aside for the interview.

When I woke up on the day set aside for the interview, I took bath after which I went to the tar road and boarded a commercial vehicle to work. When I arrived at the office I had my breakfast before walking to the third floor where the interview was scheduled to take place, to be precise at the Gambia Revenue Authority's Boardroom. Outside the Boardroom I stood for a minute before the secretary asked me to sit down on a chair that was placed outside the interview room. I sat down for some minutes and later witnessed the coming of other people who were there for the interview. To my surprise, I saw one of my former teachers on the waiting line. It was difficult for me to let him know that I was there for the same purpose even though he might have suspected that and so I pretended that I did not notice his presence. But I could not continue to pretend because we were seated in an open place where I believed that he could see me later. So I took the courage to say "Good morning sir". He responded quickly and asked if I was there for the same purpose a question that I wanted to avoid hearing. The answer was obviously "Yes sir", after which he congratulate me for my degree and I said to myself, "O God". He knew I had a degree.

While we were waiting for our turn a caller asked me to go in and as I walked in, I greeted the panel, most of whom were my co-workers, before being offered a seat. Then for a moment I introduced myself, even though most of them knew me already. This was followed by a series of questions from different members of the panel and I took my time to answer their questions to the best of my ability. After the interview, I walked out of the room and passed quietly by my former teacher wondering what he would think of. A few days later, I received a call that my application for the position of Human Resource Manager was successful and that I should collect my appointment letter from the Records Office at the Gambia Revenue Authority. After receiving the news, I went to collect my appointment letter and walked back to my office where I wrote my acceptance letter for the position as part of the requirement, and submitted it to the Records Office. A little while later, I received congratulations from many of my co-workers at the time.

After work, I went to the ghetto where I told the boys that I had been appointed to the position of Human Resource and Admin Manager at the Gambia Revenue Authority. They could not understand the point very well until I explained what the Gambia Revenue Authority is all about. Then later everyone was happy, shouting and smiling. Some embraced me with joy. However, it took me some time to move to my new office where I expected new roles and better responsibilities even though that did not just happen as I expected. Anyway, despite the unfortunate situation, I keep moving and was never a dormant person in the office, but one who always engaged on something productive, especially writing.

As time went by like most of my colleagues at work the chance arose for me to travel once gain to the United kingdom for a two- week course on succession planning and talent management at RIPA International in London. Thank God it was the then Director General of Customs & Excise Department, the late Momodou Kabba Tambajang, who was appointed as the Commissioner General of the Gambia Revenue Authority and so he approved my two- week course to RIPA in London based on my competency manifested at work. To go back to London was like going back to my city and so I had the confidence that I would be able to make it. On my departure day and before I left for Banjul International Airport I told my colleagues at the ghetto that I was to land at Heathrow Airport instead of Gatwick that I travelled to and from for so many times during the period of my studies. To be precise, I left home at 7: 10 pm and arrived at the Banjul International Airport at 7: 35pm when the flight was to take off at 8:00 pm. I thought that to arrive at the airport at that time would be ideal but to my surprise even though there were twenty-five minutes left for the flight to take off, I was asked to be at the airport earlier the next time that I was to travel.

It was a Sabena Airline that I joined and the flight only took off some minutes after 8pm that night for a night journey to London via Brussels. We arrived at Brussels after 6 hours of flying where passengers for London were asked to change flight to Heathrow, Airport in London. Upon arrival at Heathrow I went through the usual immigration check-up before being able to go out of the terminal building. Outside the terminal building, I saw my host who was there to collect me to Oxbridge in London. It only took me that night to discover that the city of London was as busy as I knew and so I was prepared for the life. I went through a very effective and enjoyable two-week course on succession planning and talent management in London where every student had full participation in the class. It was also a trip that enabled me to see different places around the city of London especially in "Victoria", which was my route to South Chelsea College during my studies in London. The trip also provided me with new knowledge, skills and experience that I could transmit to anyone who was willing to take it. It also helped me to realize my belief that "hard work pays well" especially when I met with some of my fellow countrymen that I knew during my degree programme in the UK. During the short discussions I took the opportunity to inform them that they should return to Banjul after studies so that together we could develop our beautiful country.

All the same, I left Heathrow Airport in the United Kingdom to return to Banjul via Brussels. The journey from London to Brussels lasted for 25 minutes even though it was initially predicted for fifteen minutes. According to the flight information, the delay was due to a bad weather condition. Upon arrival at Brussels, passengers to Banjul changed flight to the one for Banjul. It took us six hours from Brussels to Banjul via Dakar, the Senegalese capital, where we had an hour's stop. However when the flight took off from Dakar for Banjul, I felt glad that we were entering the Smiling Coast of Africa. The flight was not flying far and so I could see the beautiful Gambian river at a distance. It is so beautiful to view the river Gambia at a distance on a flight. Once you pass the River Gambia you are near Banjul International Airport and that was the same way we did before an announcement was made for passengers to fasten their belts in preparation for landing.

It only took me a day off from work before I submitted my report from the Succession Planning and Talent Management Course at RIPA international in London to the late Commissioner General of the Gambia Revenue Authority Mr. Momodou Kabba Tambajang. At work I was welcomed as usual by many, especially the junior staff who are always my friends. I could not believe that I was confronted by many of this category for not informing them of my travel to London. As I apologized to all, I asked myself that I was only two weeks away and most of the junior staff missed me. All the same, I have a great love for all the staff at the Gambia Revenue Authority.

As I walked back to my office I started to reason about two things: words said by many junior staff at GRA and those of friends in the UK. While thinking about the trip, I told myself that most Gambian students in London would want to return home after their studies to contribute towards national development. As I continued to remember colleagues at RIPA International in UK as well as fellow Gambians I met, I took a move to use the internet to send messages to friends in London, the content of which included telling them that I had arrived home safely. Indeed the trip to London was an opportunity for me to meet my old friends and made new friends who I said to them that The Gambia is the Smiling Coast of Africa where they needed to visit. I told them that the Gambia is a beautiful country where people of different faiths live together in peace. To confirm my point I deem it necessary to introduce the reader to my next chapter about the Gambia.

8

The Gambia, a beacon of hope

As some Gambians moved in search of a better life, particularly in the second republic I deem it necessary to give a brief history of the country to help the reader understand the long struggle the country and its people embarked on to get to the point people looked-for. Gambians have always demonstrated hard work, especially in agriculture which is the backbone of the economy. However, it was sad that after all the hard work Gambians did on their farms the people previously earned little or nothing from their farm products due to lack of access to a better market. It was the reason the people were faced with serious economic hardship that forced many youth to look for alternative means to survive. Because many Gambians were faced with numerous difficulties in terms of feeding, shelter and paying school fees, many youth decided to embark on the perilous back journey in search of better life and to help their people back in the Gambia.

The Gambia is one of Africa's smallest countries located on the western coast of Africa surrounded on three sides by the Republic of Senegal. The Gambia is the official name of the country and it was named after the River Gambia, which flows from the east to the west for three hundred miles across the entire length of the country. The country is situated on a sandy peninsula between the mouths of the Gambia River and the Atlantic Ocean. The capital, Banjul, was founded by the British as Bathurst in 1816 and was used as a base for suppressing the slave trade. The country changed the name of its capital from Bathurst to Banjul in 1973, eight years after its independence. Though considered as the smallest country in Africa with a total area of 4,363 square miles (11,300 square kilometres), the country continues to produce some of the best brains in the world with its citizens servicing in various international institutions ,including the International Criminal Court (ICC) and the United Nations. The country has enjoyed long spells of stability since independence thanks to the Creator.

The country has the typical climate conditions; thus it has a rainy season from June to October and a dry season for the rest of the year. It has a relatively flat land with its lowest point being sea level at the Atlantic Ocean with the maximum elevation being 174 feet (53 metres) in the surrounding low hills. The country has a beautiful and navigable river which is the dominant geographical feature of the country as people continue to use it both as a useful means of transportation and irrigation as well as a rich ground for fishing, boating and sailing. There is cultural diversity in the country which is backed by strong love for one another. Strong cultural beliefs continue to help the people in the promotion of togetherness for the interest of peace and stability. This is the reason the Gambia remain a model and a beacon of hope for those who look for such humanitarian gestures.

Unfortunately, Gambians has over the years experienced human rights abuses during the dictatorship rule of the Ex-President of the Second Republic. The human rights abuse has greatly affected the lives of the people, including some personnel of the security services. This was sad considering the fact that the country has peace loving people who are generous and committed to rendering humanitarian services to others who are in need. Like other countries in Africa, the Gambia has various ethnic groups that are all living in peace and harmony. This is the reason people were free to exercise their religious and cultural traditions without having the fear of getting attacked as it was the case in the second republic when the leadership almost takes full charge of religious matters.

Despite the fact that Muslims account for about 90 per cent of the population, there is religious tolerance in the country thus different faiths work hand in hand in the interest of peace and humanity. It is interesting to see how these faiths live side by side, especially during feasts like Tobaski, Koriteh and Christmas. In order to strengthen relationships between ethnic groups, Gambians continue to have inter- marriage. Different faiths in the country advocate marriage between men and women. This is important because all faiths have the belief that God created the world and brings human beings to the earth to worship him in order that they might develop and rule on this earth. To achieve this, humanity must preserve itself, living and growing, cultivating, and engaging in other meaningful acts and above all devote time to worship God. It is undeniable that the Creator has placed certain aptitude and force in human beings so that people are forced to engage in activities that will guarantee their existence.

It is in line with these beliefs that Gambians embraced the idea of marriage between men and women. In The Gambia marriage is regulated either by customary, Shari' a (Muslim), or general law. Customary law is reserved for all non-Muslims and covers inheritance, land tenure, tribal and clan leadership, as well as other relationships. Shari' a law is primary for Muslims and covers marriage and divorce. General Law is based on British law. As peace-loving people Gambians continue to condemn rape and view having affairs after marriage as illegal. In fact the people believe in the teachings of traditional values which advocate marriage among other things. This is the reason any person who is believed to have carnal knowledge of a girl under the age of 16 is considered guilty of a crime (except in the course of marriage). Incest is also illegal. Based on the beliefs of the teachings of the Quran many Muslim men in the country practise polygamy and women in monogamous unions have property and other rights, including the right to divorce their husbands. The majority of the Muslim communities continue to use Shari' a law in cases of divorce and inheritance matters.

As a democratic country, men and women have equal opportunities in many areas including employment. The government has strong belief in the employment of disabled people and because of this there are many disabled people working. In addition, there is lot of women in high positions, including the cabinet and National Assembly with a woman as the Speaker. The country has a female Vice President who has vast experiences in governance issues. Apart from the promotion of equal employment opportunities there are no statutory discrimination existing in other kinds of occupations such as mechanic and driving commercial vehicle for a living. In addition there are several women who are engaged in food vending or subsistence farming which continue to enhance their living.

Though English is the official language of the country, Gambians speak other international languages including French which is spoken in the neighbouring sister countries like Senegal, Mali and Mauritania. Because Gambians believe in living in harmony they greet each other at any time of the day and night. The most popular way of greeting in the country is the Islamic greeting Asalaamu Aleikum which means peace be on to you. The citizens are recognized all over the world for their love for peace, hospitality and sharing of their food with everyone, especially visitors. The Gambia is among the few countries in the world where citizens feel happy to share food with visitors and people passing-by.

There are many foreigners in the country who continues to enjoy peace. It was the reason majority of them engaged in business. The move was possible because the coalition government has created the enabling environment for businesses to grow. In fact the country has a beautiful port which was used by many businesspersons to bring their containers. The port of Banjul continues to be jammed with containers and vehicles due to the free atmosphere of trade created by the coalition government. In addition, various goods move in transit to the surrounding countries, especially Mali. The move helps the country earn the desired revenue and also enhances economic relationships within the sub- region. In fact having business dealing within the sub region is important because history has connected us. It is important to know that The Gambia was once part of the Mali and Kaabu Empires. The first written accounts of the region came from records of Arab traders in the 9th and 10th centuries AD. Arab traders established the trans-Saharan trade route for slaves, gold, and ivory. In the 15th century, the Portuguese took over this trade using maritime routes. At that time The Gambia was part of the Kingdom of Mali.

In 1588, the claimant to the Portuguese throne, Antonio Prior of Crato, sold exclusive trade rights on the Gambia River to English merchants: this grant was confirmed by letters patent from Queen Elizabeth I. In 1618, King James 1 granted a charter to a British company to trade with The Gambia and the Gold Coast (which is now referred to as Ghana). During the late 17th century and throughout the 18th, England and France struggled tirelessly for political and commercial supremacy in the regions of the Senegal and Gambia rivers. The 1783 Treaty of Versailles gave Great Britain possession of The Gambia, but the French retained a tiny enclave at Albreda on the north bank of the river, which was ceded to the United Kingdom in 1857.

It was a belief that during the era of the slave trade as many as three million slaves might have been taken from the region during the three centuries that the transatlantic slave trade operated. It is not known how many slaves were taken by Arab traders prior to and simultaneous with the transatlantic slave trade. Most of those taken were sold to Europeans by other Africans: some were prisoners of intertribal wars; some were sold because of unpaid debts, while others were kidnapped. Slaves were initially sent to Europe to work as servants until the market for labour expanded in the West Indies and North America in the 18th century. In 1807, slave trading was abolished throughout the British Empire, and the British tried unsuccessfully to end the slave traffic in The Gambia. They established the military post of Bathurst (now Banjul) in1816. In the ensuing years, Banjul was under the jurisdiction of the British governor general in Sierra Leone. In 1888, The Gambia became a separate colonial entity.

The 1889 agreement with France established the present boundaries, and The Gambia became a British Crown Colony, divided for administrative purposes into the colony (city of Banjul and the surrounding area) and the protectorate (remainder of the territory). The Gambia received its own executive and legislative councils in 1901 and gradually progressed towards self -government. 1906 ordinance abolished slavery. During World War II, the pace of constitutional reform quickened. Following general elections in 1962, full internal self -government was granted in 1963. The Gambia achieved independence on 18 February 1965 as a constitutional monarchy within the British Commonwealth. Shortly thereafter, the government proposed conversion from a monarchy to a republic with an elected president replacing the British monarch as chief of state. The proposal failed to receive the two-thirds majority required to amend the constitution, but the results won widespread attention abroad as testimony to The Gambia's observance of secret balloting, free elections and civil rights and liberties. On 24 April 1970, The Gambia became a republic following a referendum.

The country's independence on 18 February 1965 marked a turning point in its history as Gambian's became more unified under the umbrella of peace and harmony. The independence brought about a moment of reflection and joy because people were able to think about where they were and where they would love to be in the future. Because colonialism had a serious negative impact on Gambians it becomes important for the present and future generations of the country to know their history and work together to develop the country.

Each time I sit to think about The Gambia under the Commonwealth from 1962 until 1970 with Elizabeth II having a say in the affairs of the country and Sir Dawda Kairaba Jawara as the Prime Minister and Head of Government I question the freedom of the people at the time. It was amazing to know that The Gambia only became a Republic in 1970, after a referendum, thus paving way for the country to have its first President, Sir Dawda Kairaba Jawara. The country's first President was born on 16 May 1924 at Barajally Village; McCarthy Island Division (now Central River Region). He was a veterinary surgeon who served as a veterinary officer for some time. Mr. Jawara travelled the length and breadth of the Gambia during the period for vaccinating cattle. It was in that process that he established social contacts and cordial relationships with many cattle owners in locations referred to as protectorate areas. He reaped the fruits of good relationship as the majority of the cattle owners and chiefs became his initial political supporters.

Sir Dawda Kairaba Jawara, 1st President of the Gambia

Prior to joining politics, Sir Dawda was studying abroad. The former head of state returned to The Gambia in 1953 after completing his studies. At the time of his return to the country, politics in the colony were dominated by a group of urban elite from Bathurst and Kombo St. Mary's area. It was in a meeting held at Basse in 1959 where the leadership of the People's Progressive Society made a name change which was aimed at challenging the urban-based parties and their leaders. The move led to the birth of the Protectorate People's Party. It was in the same year that a delegation headed by Sanjally Bojang, the founding member of a new party, together with Bokarr Fofana and Madiba Janneh came to Abuko and informed Dawda Kairaba Jawara about his nomination as Secretary of the Party. The development forced Jawara to resign from his position as Chief Veterinary Officer purposely with the intention to contest 1960 election. And it was in the same year that the Protectorate People's Party was renamed People's Progressive Party (PPP). Jawara's party was able to supersede the urban-based parties and their leaders. His participation in politics and subsequently defeat of the urban-based parties was what Arnold Hughes referred to as "Green Revolution" in his words it means a political process in which a rural elite emerged to challenge and eventually defeat an urban-based political party.

With Jawara's rise to power, the colonial administration began gradual withdrawal from The Gambia. This marked the Gambia's peaceful transition from colonial rule. The country's independence had serious challenges due to lack of development during colonial rule. It is sad to know that many African countries had evolved economies that were seriously vulnerable and heavily dependent on colonial markets and former colonial powers. Of course the expectation of the people after independence was that Sir Dawda Kairaba Jawara and his government would quickly build the country and develop a strong economy capable of sustaining both the farmers and urban dwellers. Gambians generally had the hope that political independence would bring immediate improvement in their lives. It was not a surprise that the high hope was influenced by the promises made to the people by various political parties, including the People's Progressive Party.

While in that situation a disgruntled ex-politician called Kukoi Samba Sanyang and some members of the Field Force attempted a failed coup in 1981 to oust the PPP regime. The failed coup followed serious weakening of the country's economy and accusation of corruption against some leading politicians under the PPP government. It was carried out on 30 July 1981 by the National Revolutionary Council composed of Kukoi Samba Sanyang's Social and Revolutionary Labour Party (SRLP) together with some elements of the Field Force.

The attempted coup reflected the need for change at least to some civilians and their friends in the Field Force. It was believed that the hegemony of the PPP contraction of intra-party competition and growing social inequalities were factors that could be discounted. Also Kukoi and his team believed that the reason for the aborted coup was due to the worsening economy whose major victims were the urban youth. In his 1981 New Year message to the nation Sir Dawda Jawara explained the Gambia's economic problems thus: "We live in a world saddled with massive economic problems. The economic situation has generally been characterized by rampant inflation, periods of excessive monetary instability and credit squeeze....soaring oil prices and commodity speculation. These worldwide problems have imposed extreme limitations on the economies like The Gambia".

The aborted coup which was partly a result of the Senegalese intervention to restore Jawara to power created an agreement between The Gambia and Senegal as President Jawara and President Diouf of Senegal, at a joint press conference, announced plans for the establishment of the Senegambia Confederation. Five months after the aborted coup, the treaties of confederation were signed by the Gambia and Senegal in the Senegalese capital, Dakar. Sir Dawda Kairaba Jawara encountered serious pressure due to the outcome of the aborted coup. Under the treaty with Senegal, President Diouf served as President and Sir Dawda as his Vice President. This followed the setting up of a confederal parliament and cabinet with several ministerial positions going to the Gambia.

In addition, a new Gambian Army was established as part of a new confederate army. Up to the time of change of government there had been very little change in the structure of the economy which remained very heavily dependent on groundnut production. Agriculture and tourism are the dominant sectors and also the main sources of foreign exchange, employment, and income for the country. Once the Gambia realized its growing economy, the government in 1970 introduced the policy of Gambianization, which led to an expansion of the state's role in the economy.

In 1985 The Gambia initiated the Economic Recovery Programme (ERP), one of the most comprehensive economic adjustment programmes devised by counties in sub-saharan Africa. With the help of a team from the Harvard Institute for International Development and the International Monetary Fund, the Gambia greatly reformed the economic structure of the country. Under the ERP, money-seeking opportunities became more abundant, and many private businessmen and public officials turned to illegal means to make profit. Several cases of corruption were revealed which seriously indicted the PPP regime. The Gambia Commercial and Development Bank (GCDB) collapsed mainly due to its failure to collect loans. An asset Management and Recovery Corporation (AMRC) was established under an Act of Parliament in 1992, but the PPP government was not willing to use its influence to assist AMRC in its recovery exercise. In an embezzlement scheme at the Gambia Cooperative Union (GCU), fraud was revealed in Customs, and through the process of privatization it was discovered that many dummy loans had been given to well-connected individuals at GCDB. A group of Parastatal heads and big businessmen closely associated with the PPP referred to as the "Banjul Mafia" were seen as the culprits responsible for the corruption in the public sector.

Driven to make profit many elites did not refrain from manipulating state power to maintain a lifestyle of wealth and privilege. By 1992 the Gambia was rated as one of the poorest countries in Africa with a 45 year life expectancy at birth, an infant mortality rate of 130 per 1000 live births, a child mortality rate of 292 per 1000, and an under-five mortality rate of 227 per 1000. At that time, 120 out of every 1000 live births died of malaria. The Gambia also had a 75 per cent illiteracy rate, only 40 percent of the population had access to potable water supply, and over 75 per cent of the population was living in absolute poverty.

The structural adjustment programmes implemented in response to the economic crises resulted in government segmentation, privatization, less patronage in co-opting various groups and growing corruption. The 30 years of the PPP regime operated within limited resources coupled with high level of corruption made it impossible for the PPP to bring about lots of developments in the country. Towards the end of the People's Progressive Party rule alongside the post-coup revelations and enquiries suggest that corruption was both a significant phenomenon and one which played an important role in the PPP's survival. Sir Dawda Kairaba Jawara had a clear understanding of the political advantages of corruption. Corruption in the PPP regime formed an important component of the patronage network facilitating the elite's accumulation of wealth. The move provided the means of creating and maintaining mutually beneficial and supportive relationship between PPP politicians under Jawara, senior civil servant and some Gambian businesspeople.

The practice of corruption by some officials of the PPP has undermined the regime. Again as the country struggled with the economy Kukoi Samba Sanyang told Gambians that corruption and the squandering of public funds were the primary motive of intervention even though Gambians don't believe in the use of guns to change government. There was no doubt about the strong element of opportunism in Sanyang's actions, yet the fact that Kukoi took upon corruption as a suitable justification for his actions reflected increasing public awareness of the problem. Less than a month before the coup, the Reverend Ian Roach spoke out publicly against corruption. The local press reported numerous instances of low-level bureaucratic theft, and higher up Jawara's leniency towards his ministers and civil servants towards the end of the 1970s was widely resented.

The increased public awareness of corruption weakened the People's Progressive Party regime and furnished the 1994 coup d'etat. Many soldiers reportedly regarded their bad living conditions as a manifestation of corruption under the PPP regime. People voiced his weakness in dealing with corruption and because of the accusation Jawara responded saying: "I believe in the rule of law and democracy. We are a poor country where petty jealousies exist. One buys a car or builds a house, so he must be corrupt, and Sir Dawda Kairaba Jawara did not do anything. I am expected to serve as a judge and policeman at the same time. At the Cooperative Union it was agreed that a Presidential Commission be established to investigate alleged corruption. Action was taken, and then the coup occurred. We must let the law take its course. We were serious to run a government according to the rule of law and for this we were highly rated and respected". However, it is important to know that the first republic registered significant developments as they built schools and health centres. The regime also made developments in the area of infrastructure and agriculture. The regime could have done better but it was not possible due to the corrupt practices of some senior civil servants that took advantage of President Jawara lenience.

However, the first republic conducted rehabilitation of the ports around Half-Die which followed the official opening by Sir Dawda Kairaba Jawara in November 1974. The move was made possible through the support of the International Development Association of the World Bank, Balfour Beatty and Company Ltd, Maunselland Partners, the Gambia Ports Authority and the Ministry of Works and Communications. At the handing over ceremony the Minister of Works and Communications at the time Mr. Alhaji Sir Alieu S. Jack, said the development of the Gambia Ports must be seen in the overall perspective of the improvement of infrastructure throughout the country. Mr. Robert Madi Chairman of the Board of Directors of the Gambia Ports Authority told the gathering that the berth and facilities that the Authority had to offer made them hopeful that the ports would attract more shipping companies around the world.

The overall cost of the project was more than D 7,115,000 in 1972. Work on Ports project began in May 1972 following the award of the contract to Balfour Beatty and Co. Ltd. The project was financed through a World Bank loan. The 400 foot berth which was provided was said to accommodate one large vessel with a draught of up to 36 feet. Other facilities provided included an enclosed Customs Office with two transit sheds of a total aggregate covered area of about 54,000 square feet at the Admiralty Wharf site, bunkering and petroleum delivery facilities. The PPP regime also did some improvement to Government Wharf and the construction of two moving dolphins.

Until a military coup in July 1994, The Gambia was led by President Sir Dawda Kairaba Jawara, who was re-elected five times in office. The relative stability of the Jawara era was first broken by a violent, unsuccessful coup attempt in 1981 led by Kukoi Samba Sanyang who, on two occasions, had unsuccessfully sought election to parliament. After a week of violence which left several hundred dead, President Jawara, while in London during the attack, appealed to the Senegalese government for military assistance. In the aftermath of the attempted coup, the Republic of Senegal and The Gambia signed the 1982 Treaty of Confederation. The Senegambia confederation aimed to combine the armed forces of the two nations and to unify their economies and currencies. The Gambia however withdrew from the confederation in 1989.

Yahya Jammeh, 2ND President of the Gambia

In July 1994, the Armed Forces seized power in a military coup d'etat. The new government was headed by Lieutenant Yahya A J J Jammeh who doubled as the Chairman. He was born on 25 May 1965 in Kanilai Village, Foni Kansala, in the year when The Gambia became free from its colonial master. He attended Gambia High School and was later enlisted in the Gambia National Army in 1984. Yahya Jammeh became an escort training officer, National Police Training School in 1987, army cadet officer in 1987 and second lieutenant in 1989. He was in charge of presidential escort, presidential Guards from 1989 to 1990 and then became a high-ranking member of the Gambia Military Police from 1990 to 1994. Yahya Jammeh assumed the post of Chairman of the Armed Forces Provisional Ruling Council in 1994. He became an elected president of the Republic of the Gambia following a successful election held in 1996.

The AFPRC announced a transition plan for a return to democratic civilian government. The Provisional Independent Electoral Commission (PIEC) was established in 1996 to conduct national elections. The transition process included the compilation of a new electoral register, adoption of a new constitution by referendum in August 1996, and Presidential and Legislative elections in September 1996 and January 1997 respectively. After the election, Retired Col. Yahya A J J Jammeh was sworn into office as President of the Republic of The Gambia in November 1996. The PIEC was transformed to the Independent Electoral Commission (IEC) in 1997 and became responsible for the registration of voters and conduct of elections and referenda.

It was some time in 2001 and early in 2002 when The Gambia completed a full cycle of presidential, legislative, and local elections, which foreign observers considered free, fair and transparent. President Yahya Jammeh, who was re-elected, took the oath of office on 21 December 2001. The APRC maintained its strong majority in the National Assembly; particularly after the main opposition United Democratic Party (UDP) boycotted the legislative elections. President Jammeh was re-elected for a third 5 -year term on 22 September 2006 with 67% of the vote. The UDP received 27% of the vote, and instead of boycotting future elections, vowed to take part in the 2007 National Assembly elections in which the ruling Alliance for Patriotic Reorientation and Construction (APRC) won 42 of the available 48 elected seats.

The 1970 constitution, which divided the government into executive, legislative and judicial branches, was suspended after the 1994 military coup. And as part of the transition process, the AFPRC established the Constitution Review Commission (CRC) through a decree in March 1995. In accordance with the timetable for the transition to a democratically-elected government, the commission drafted a new constitution for The Gambia which was approved in a referendum in August 1996. The constitution provides for a strong presidential government, a legislative, an independent judiciary, and the protection of human rights.

It is important to know that local government in The Gambia varies. The capital city, Banjul and the larger Kanifing municipality have elected town and municipal councils. Five rural regions exist, each with a council containing a majority of elected members. Each council has its own treasury and is responsible for local government services. District chiefs retain traditional powers authorized by customary law in some instances. The Gambia was one of the oldest existing multi -party democracies in Africa before and after the July 1994 coup d'etat. The country conducted elections every five years since independence. However after the military coup, politicians from the deposed government and other senior government officials were banned from participating in politics until July 2001.

A presidential election was held in September 1996, in which Retired Col. Yahya AJ J Jammeh won 56% of the vote. The legislative elections held in January 1997 were dominated by the APRC which captured 33 out of 45 seats. In July 2001, the ban on Jawara-era political parties and politicians was lifted. Four registered opposition parties participated in the 18 October 2001 presidential election, which the incumbent President Yahya Jammeh won with almost 53% of the votes. President Jammeh won the September 2006 elections with 67% of the vote while the opposition alliance won a total of 27%.

Adama Barrow, 3rd President of the Gambia

However, The Gambia saw a change of government through the ballot box on 1 December 2016 thus bringing into power Mr. Adama Barrow, the standard bearer of the Coalition. Mr. Barrow officially assumed the mantle of leadership on 19 January 2017 after he was sworn-in in Dakar, Senegal as the President of the Republic of the Gambia following the political impasse that followed the presidential election in December 2016. Mr. Barrow's election to power marked the end of Yahya Jammeh's 22 years of rule. Mr. Adama Barrow was born on Friday 15 February 1965 in Mankamang Kunda, a small village in Jimara Upper River Region. The village is a few kilometers away from Basse the regional capital of the country. He attended Koba Kunda Primary School in URR, Crab Island Secondary School and Muslim High School in Banjul. He was brought up by Alhaji Mousa Njie in Banjul in the Wollof Community at Old Perseverance Street. Mousa Njie was from Julangel in the Upper River Region.

After the completion of his education in the Gambia, Mr. Barrow joined Alhagie Musa & Sons business where he worked for several years before becoming the Sales Manager. Adama Barrow later proceeded to the United Kingdom in 2000 to further his studies. While in the UK, Mr. Barrow worked as a security Guard at Argos store in Holloway Road, North London so as to raise money that could be used to support him. After acquiring a degree in real estate, he returned to the Gambia in 2006. In order to fully utilize his Real Estate degree, Mr. Barrow established his own business referred to as, Majum Real Estate and served as the Chief Executive Officer of the said business.

Adama Barrow has Mandinka, Fulla and Sarahule backgrounds as his father; Mamudu Barrow is from a Mandinka Tribe while his Mother, Kaddijatou Jallow, is from a Fulla Tribe. Adama was brought up by a Sarahule Man who undoubtedly contributed to his success in Education and Business. Mr. Barrow has two wives, Fatou Bah and Sarjo Mballow and he is blessed with five children at the time of being on the spotlight in the political spectrum of the Gambia. As demonstrated during the 2016 political campaign, Adama Barrow's coming into the political spectrum marked a new era of political realities in the Gambia. Not only did he have the support of the people as a standard bearer of the Coalition but many admired him because he is humble, kind and always demonstrate maturity in the way in behaves both at the political platform and private life. Mr. Barrow was a long time member of the united democratic party (UDP) and has contested in the Parliamentary elections in the Jimara constituency but never won any of the elections. While in the United Democratic Party (UDP), he served as Treasurer in 2013. Despite his previous participation in parliamentary elections, lot of people said Mr. Barrow was not among the household names in The Gambia prior to becoming the standard bearer of the Coalition. All the same, he is the choice of hundreds of thousands of electorates in the country as indicated in the 2016 election results.

Undoubtedly, Mr. Barrow was however put into the political limelight at the United Democratic Party following the imprisonment of the Party leader Lawyer Ousainou N Darboe and many of his executives. Many believed that his nomination at party level and subsequent selection through democratic way to head the Coalition was a blessing for the opposition political parties and their sympathizers who for many years yearned for a change of government through the ballot box. To help the reader with accurate information about Adama Barrow, I deem it necessary to state following point about him:

- Born on 15 February 1965 at Mankamang Kunda in the Jimara District, Upper River Region
- Education, Koba Kunda School, URR, Crab Island Secondary School and Muslim High School in Banjul.   Degree in Real Estate, in London, UK
- Brought up by Alhaji Mousa Njie in Banjul in the Wollof Community at Old Perseverance Street
- Mamudu Barrow, his father from a Mandinka Tribe
- Kaddijatou Jallow, his mother from a Fulla Tribe

- He has two wives, Fatou Bah and Sarjo Mballow
- He is blessed with five children
- He was United Democratic Party treasurer in 2013
- He was Chief Executive officer, Majum Real Estate
- He was UDP standard bearer in 2016 before the formation of the Coalition
- He later stood as Independent in 2016 following his resignation from the UDP to enable him lead the Coalition
- He was elect the President on 1 December 2016
- He is devoted Muslim who is truthful and honest.

His key campaign promises are:

1. To return The Gambia to its membership of the Commonwealth of Nations,
2. The International Criminal Court (ICC)
3. Unified the divided people
4. To reform the Security Services; better pay
5. To guarantee stability of tenure in the job (eradicate fear element among the workforce)
6. To Create employment (build factories & companies)
7. To lift economy, thus enhancing living standard of the people
8. To give value to education (knowledgeable people to get employment)
9. To Promote democracy and respect the rule of law
10. To promote freedom of speech
11. To set up a temporary transition government formed members from the coalition
12. To step down at the end of his three year term as contained in the Memorandum of Understanding of the Coalition.

It is not a surprise that following many years of British colonial rule in the Gambia, Western food is available in the country. Gambian traditional food includes benachin (Jollof rice, a mixture of spiced meat and rice cooked with tomato puree and vegetables), base nyebe (rice stew of chicken or beef with green beans and other vegetables), chere (steamed millet flour balls), domoda (meat or chicken stewed in groundnut butter and served with rice), plasas (meat and smoked fish cooked in palm oil with green vegetables served with fu-fu (mashed cassava), and chura-ger teh (a sweet porridge which consists of pounded groundnuts and rice with yoghurt or sour milk). In The Gambia the most popular eaten fruits are mangoes, bananas, grapefruit, papayas, and oranges.

Following the change of government through the ballot box, the government of the Gambia continues to commit in ensuring a private sector-led and market-determined pricing policy and liberalized agricultural commodity input and output marketing in order to ensure a regular supply and timely availability of important management of inputs on a demand-driven basis and also fetch remunerative prices for farmers' produce.

In the Gambia, Agriculture, which is the backbone of the country, continues to be given a lot of attention by the coalition government. It is a fact to say that agriculture is one of the most viable sources of food and income for most of the Gambian population, as 75 % of the country's labour force is actively engaged in this crucial sector for their living. It is also responsible for an estimated two-thirds of the total household income. This significant contribution makes the sector attractive to both public and private investment. The agriculture sector continues to engage in the actualization of the mentioned policy objectives.

About 70 per cent of the Gambia's population is comprised of subsistence farmers and the majority of these are women. Groundnuts make up the majority of export products. There are also lots of millet growers in the country. The country has very few manufacturing companies and because of this it has liberal trade policies and continues to encourage tourism. The private sector of the economy is led by tourism, trading and fisheries. The Gambia's economy is heavily based on agriculture, with an estimated 70 per cent of the population depending on it for food, employment and cash income. The main cash products are groundnuts, cotton, horticulture and livestock, while subsistence crops are composed of cereals such as millet, sorghum, maize and rice. Agriculture contributes between 20 and 30% of the Gross Domestic Product (GDP) and generates almost 90 % of domestic export earnings. In this context, agricultural development is critical to present and future economic growth and improvements in the welfare of The Gambia.

The elements of climate, land and water that constitute the main agricultural resources base of the country reflect what the potential farming system can be. The climate is Sudano-Sahalian with a short rainy season from June to October and a long dry season from November to May. Annual rainfall varies from 900 mm in the south-west to about 500 mm in the north-east. Land availability on the other hand continues to remain a controversy until a distinction is made between "physical" and "economic" availability. It is estimated that 54% of the total land area of 1,036,534 ha is regarded as arable land of varying degrees. Additional water resources comprise an inflow of the River Gambia and two aquifer (the exploited shallow and the underutilized deep) systems underlying the entire country. The river, because of the tidal influence, is subjected to saline intrusion and the 1g/1 saline front ranges between 80 km and 250 km upstream, thereby requiring an effective water use planning for a sustainable increase in agricultural productivity.

The Department of Agricultural Services (DAS), formerly Department of Agriculture, was established in 1923 with the mandate of improving the quality of the groundnuts grown and preparing of the groundnuts produced for export. Although the focus remained on increasing the export of the groundnut crop to earn the needed foreign exchange, the mandate of the department expanded to include food crops (millet, maize, rice, sorghum) and other cash crops (cotton and sesame). Food crops cultivated area, yield and management. The Gambia has a total land area of about 1.1 million hectares with 550,000 hectares being categorized as arable in 1994 and 157,016 hectares were cultivated by 574,749 farmers. In 2003 the total area under cultivation increased to 284, 792 hectares with, 881,146 farmers working on them. This represented a remarkable increase of 81 % and 53 % respectively. These increments in both the total cultivated area and farming population are reflective of the positive response by the general population.

In an effort to increase the national food security, only 15 % of the total arable land was used for cereal cultivation few years ago, but the figure increased to 32 %. Cereals included coarse grains, early and late millet, sorghum and maize and paddy rice. Total area cultivated of coarse grains increased from 68,766 hectares to 155,667 hectares in 2003, representing a huge increase of 126 %. In the wake of these massive increments, 61 % was under the cultivation of early millet. Cereal yield increased from 1,122 kg/ha to 1,230 kg/ha, a rise of 9.6 %. This increase, apart from the part played by the low production per area, is greatly influenced by the unfavourable weather conditions like heavy rainfall, reflective of the poor state of the soil and the endemic unaffordability of chemical fertilizers which prevents most farmers from using them. Cereals are the most crucial group of food crops that are consumed by households in the country and they contribute over 50 % of the total energy supply while animal protein, fats and edible oils constitute only 20 % of the total energy requirement. Cereal production has seen a tremendous increase over the years. Production has gone from 95,332 metric tons to 213,337 metric tons, an increment of 124 % over a period of 9 years. Much of the expansion of the total cereal management emanated from the early millet management, representing 50 % of the cereal management. With regard to the national food security, commercial food imports and aid, the cereal balance sheet for The Gambia has shown that the total cereal requirement in 2003 was estimated at 245,400 metric tons, showing a national food surplus of 45,480 metric tons.

Rice cultivation does not only satisfy the population in terms of food security but it is a primary staple food for most of the Gambian population. In this regard, rice is grown in two broad rice ecologies that exist in the Gambia and these are upland and lowland rice growing areas. The erratic rainfall experienced over the years affects upland rice cultivation as its area increased massively from 2,888 hectares to 8,862 hectares. This unprecedented increase was associated with the adoption by farmers of short-duration rice varieties, coupled with the most recently introduced drought rice variety called the New Rice for Africa (NERICA) developed by the West African Development Association (WADA) for the uplands. Upland rice management increased from 3,661 metric tons to 8,862 metric tons showing a twofold increase. The lowlands also make up part of the rice growing ecology in The Gambia and over the years swamp rice cultivation suffered from two natural calamities, namely drought and floods. The cumulative effect of these calamities resulted in an undesirable reduction of swamp rice cultivated area as well as production levels. The total area under swamp rice cultivation declined from 10,281 hectares to 6,661 in 2003, indicating a reduction of about 35 %. Similarly, about 50 % decline was registered for swamp rice production.

Horticultural production-mainly fruits and vegetable enhances, improved food security greatly through direct consumption and income generation for growers and sellers. The exports of horticultural products have increased to over D50 million over the years due to the contribution from the government and its development partners. There are two broad categories of horticultural growers that exist in the horticultural sub-sector, namely village vegetable garden schemes mainly women and commercial farms and the private sector which consists mainly of big farmers. In response to the drought condition in 2002, government and the FAO formulated a Technical Cooperation Programme (TCP) to help small-scale horticultural producers nationwide with garden equipment, watering cans, fencing materials, spades, as well as inputs like fertilizers, seeds, and agro-chemicals. Since then through the intervention of programme /projects, the sub-sector's overall performance has increased.

Studies have indicated that The Gambia stands at a comparative advantage in the management of horticultural crops. The horticulture sub-sector has provided a great deal of the requirement for fruits and vegetables in the tourist industry. The sub-sector engages over 60 % of all women farmers with more than 4,000 labourers employed in the large commercial horticultural farms. These commercial farmers are primarily engaged in cultivation for the export market. It is estimated that four hundred and ten village gardens are operational throughout the country (WR 70, LRR 63, NBR 59, CRR/N 75, CRR/S 45 and

URR 98) which supply mainly the local markets and four lumo sites: Kaur, Wassu, Brikama and Bureng .

These market outlets significantly contribute to improve the marketing of the horticultural products and also minimize post-harvest losses. To optimize the output of these sub-sectors, one hectare fruit tree orchards was established in each of the six agricultural regions, which serve as the centre of several comprehensive farmer training sessions on improved horticultural crop management techniques such as Integrated Pest Management (IPM), post -harvest handling, processing and preservation, marketing and storage as well as group management skills. Garden schemes are apparent in most parts of the regions and support to these schemes includes the provision of live fencing materials.

Cash crops are an important commodity used in The Gambia and the Ministry of Agriculture does not relent in its efforts in ensuring that the commodity meets the requirements of the people. It is for this reason that the country pays great attention to the cash crops cultivated area, yield and management. In The Gambia, groundnut is the main cash crop and it is consumed as an important food crop yet cheaper source of proteins, especially in the local diets. The area cultivated has been fluctuating annually over the years. The lowest cultivated area recorded was in 1996, which stands at about 64,413 hectares and the highest in 2001, which was 138,888 hectares. Total production has also been fluctuating annually due to the variability of the cultivated area, poor seed nuts, inadequate quantities and unaffordability of chemical fertilizers. For example, its productive capacity was estimated at 151,069 metric tons in 2001 and 71,526 metric tons the following year.

Despite the decline however, a 30 % increase in groundnut production was recorded between 2002 and 2003. Cotton, which is also a cash crop, occupies less than 3, 000 hectares on average of the overall land. Other crops such as cassava and potato occupy about 1,500 to 2,000 hectares in small garden and commercial schemes. Sesame is another increasingly important cash crop mainly grown by women's groups known as Sesame Growers' Associations (SGAS). Like groundnuts, sesame cultivation has markedly increased over the years. With the fact that the soil in The Gambia is increasingly becoming fertile, Government has accorded top priority to the provision of adequate agricultural inputs to farmers. Over the years, Government has provided agricultural inputs to farmers which are aimed at boosting their crop management and intensifying crop diversification. The Government through its technical arm (Ministry of Agriculture) bought some fertilizers and seeds for the farming communities.

Livestock production is an important complementary attribute of the Gambian farming systems. The sub-sector's contribution to the GDP was estimated at

5 per cent for 1998. Livestock consists of cattle, small ruminants and poultry, which are an important part of promoting national food security through direct consumption of the product (meat, milk, broilers and eggs) and incomes earned from the sale of animals and animal products. It contributes about 24 % of agricultural GDP with an annual growth rate of 3.3 %. This sub-sector provides most of the draught power required for crop production. It is also an important source of transportation in the rural areas, principally for the evaluation of agricultural produce to local markets. The increasing importance of the sector has been stimulated partly by macroeconomic policies that have promoted agricultural diversification (Darboe et al, 1991). Furthermore, intermittent drought concomitant with the decline in soil fertility have resulted in poor crop performance, leading farmers to diversify their production base to include livestock production. The most important species are cattle (415,843), goats (371,412), sheep (182,578), donkeys (85,962) and horses (32,268). Poultry is also important both in the peri-urban and rural areas. The number of birds is estimated to have increased from 345,000 in 1984/85 to 719,814 in 2007/2008. Only a relatively small number of pigs (population of about 24,281) are reared due to religious reasons.

The Government of The Gambia in collaboration with its development partners has made important project interventions in the livestock sub-sector. These interventions include the Integrated Rural Development Project for Livestock, Sheep and Goat Development Project (GAM 87/004), Pan-African Rinderpest Campaign, FAO Tele-Food Projects, Rural Finance Community Initiative Project and EDF Livestock programmes. The cumulative effects of these interventions impacted positively on the livestock sub-sector and resulted in increased livestock management and marketing. Cattle, small ruminants (sheep and goats) and different species of poultry are raised to generate income and supplement diets. The cattle population has stabilized at around 300,000 head while sheep and goat population fluctuated within a narrow margin averaging about 100,000 head and the poultry population increased to 800,000 birds of all species. At an estimated 8 kg per capita meat consumption and other dairy products, estimated between 10 and 24 kg per caput per annum respectively, national requirements had to be met from commercial imports.

As people's participation in agriculture was growing, I embarked on a countrywide tour in February 2017 primarily to know the levels of farmers' preparation for farming in the third republic as well as freedom of speech and movement. The tour enabled me realized that after many years of oppressive rule that almost affected every Gambians, farmers now have the liberty to talk about their plans to market their farm products without fear of being dictated by the government. I found this wonderful as it demonstrates the position of the third republic in terms of serving the interest of the people. The crucial role of government in promoting agriculture and freedom of speech made me believe in the country and its leadership. Anyone in the country would tell you the government has transformed society by empowering the people. Every Gambian needs to know that the government is committed to ensuring that people's livelihoods are enhanced as it continues to invest massively in health, education and agriculture.

However it is to be noted that for any country to attain meaningful development its people should be willing to work hard in order to feed themselves. For this reason the new government came up with a series of development programmes, particularly on agriculture and youth development. Also, the move by the leadership to visit farmers in different regions in the country should be viewed as networking and stakeholder management, thus every farmer has a stake in national building. Besides, the move helps in boosting the morale of people in what they do and in the new leadership.

One thing that every citizen should know is that it is only through collective responsibility that the country can attain food self-sufficiency. Together we can fight poverty which exists in every part of the world due to a number of factors including:
1. People's low level of earnings
2. Unnecessary wars and natural disasters like drought
3. Economic meltdown
4. Unfair distribution of the national cake
5. Intimidation and persecution

Though there are some problems affecting farmers, the government of the Gambia is in the forefront in the development of agriculture, with the Coalition government showing concerns to farmers daily. I have heard people from all walks of life talking about the importance of agriculture and each time I ask what it means I get an answer such as feed oneself and use its products for commercial benefits. To know this better I have engaged in agriculture and it has enabled me to realize the benefit of farming. There is hardly any human who lives without eating farm products and because of this, everyone should be willing to work and earn a decent living. Together Gambians should support the development programmes of the government so as to help the country realize food self-sufficiency.

The youth must take a leading role in this struggle as they form the majority of the population. Evidently, the government is working hard to promote youth development after many years of the former government's disregard for youth development. It was lack of support to youth that created the mass movement of people through the dangerous back way journey in the name of searching greener pasture. Nonetheless, it is important to know that the coalition government has two projects for youth development. The eleven (11) million Euros Youth Empowerment Project (YEP) and the 3.9 million Euros International Organization for Migration (IOM) Project provided to the coalition government are meant to address the youth empowerment in the New Gambia. With these projects Gambians are hopeful that the high rate of unemployment among the youth will be addressed.

Printed in the United States
By Bookmasters